Tom Scott was born in Glasgow in 1918. His father was a boiler-maker, and Red Clydeside was an enduring influence. His early years were spent working as a stonemason in St Andrews – the town and its 'characters' later appeared in his poem sequence *Brand the Builder*. After the Second World War, he lived in London, taking part in its literary life. His first use of Scots as a poetic language, encouraged by T.S. Eliot, was in translations of Villon. Scott returned to Scotland in 1952 and studied at Newbattle Abbey and later at Edinburgh University. His doctoral thesis on Dunbar became the basis of a published critical study, still among the standard works in the field. A socialist and a nationalist, Tom Scott wrote a number of long and complex poems in Scots. He also edited *The Oxford Book of Scottish Verse*, with John MacQueen; and *The Penguin Book of Scottish Verse*. A selection of his work, *The Collected Shorter Poems*, was published by Agenda/Chapman, Edinburgh, in 1993. Scott died in 1995.

By the same author

Poetry
Seeven Poems o Maister Francis Villon
Ode til New Jerusalem
The Ship and Ither Poems
At the Shrine o the Unkent Sodger
Brand the Builder
The Tree
The Dirty Business
Collected Shorter Poems
Oxford Book of Scottish Verse (Editor, with John MacQueen)
Late Medieval Scots Poetry (Editor)
The Penguin Book of Scottish Verse (Editor)

Criticism
Dunbar: An Exposition of the Poems

For younger readers
Tales of King Robert the Bruce
True Thomas (with Heather Scott)

Tales of
Sir William Wallace

Guardian of Scotland

Freely adapted from

THE WALLAS

of Blin Hary

by
Tom Scott

Steve Savage
LONDON AND EDINBURGH

Steve Savage Publishers Ltd
The Old Truman Brewery
91 Brick Lane
LONDON
E1 6QL

www.savagepublishers.com

Published in Great Britain by Steve Savage Publishers Ltd 2005

First published by Gordon Wright Publishing Ltd 1981
Copyright © Tom Scott 1981, 1997

ISBN-13: 978-1-904246-16-9
ISBN-10: 1-904246-16-8

British Library Cataloguing in Publication Data
A catalogue entry for this book is available from the British Library.

Typeset by Steve Savage Publishers Ltd

Printed and bound by The Cromwell Press Ltd

CONTENTS

Our antecessowris that we suld of rede
And hald in mynde thar nobille deid
We lat ourslide throw werray sleuthfulness
And castis us euir till uthir besynes...
We reid of ane rycht famouss of renowne.
Of worthi blude that ryngis in this regioune
And hensfurth I will my process hald
Of Wilyham Wallas yhe haf hard beyne tald.

PREFACE

We know very little about Hary the Minstrel, or Blin Hary. John Major tells us he was blind from birth and that he composed *The Wallas* some time between 1470 and 1480. There are a few entries in the *High Treasurer's Accounts* of sums paid to 'Blin Hary' for reciting poems to James IV and his court, the last of these being dated 1492. Dunbar names him among the dead in his *Lament for the Makaris* before the name of Patrick Johnstoun who died in 1494. Hary himself tells us in the text of his poem, which is just under 12,000 lines, that he is a burel (uneducated) man, and that his poem is derived from a Latin original, presumably in prose, by John Blair, which is part of our lost literature. But if Hary was blind, he must have had an educated translator to help him with the Latin.

As an unfortunate and handicapped man, Hary must have come under the care and charity of the Church, and from Homer down, there is a tradition of teaching blind people to memorise and recite poems and tales as a means of livelihood more dignified than straight begging. Certainly there is high art in Hary's poem at its best, and there is no art without intensive schooling: undoubtedly he would learn the tales and the technique of telling them by oral instruction.

At the end of the poem, Hary mentions Bishop Sinclair of Dunkeld in relation to the Blair book, saying that Sinclair 'gat this book and confermd it himsell / For verray true'. Sinclair had intended sending it to the Pope. Later on, Hary remarks that although many better poets than himself had 'reigned' in Scotland, none of them did their duty by Wallace, leaving that task to his own poor hands.

Given the above, it is not surprising that the poem is a rag-bag of various tales loosely strung together with little or no regard for chronology. Anyone such as Hary might have earned his supper by reciting one of these or one or two together, perhaps by request of his audience. This, plus the lack of visual accuracy, or even probability, makes the whole poem a translator's nightmare. I have done my best with it, but cannot claim to have achieved the impossible.

The merit of Blin Hary's work, its uniqueness, with passages of excellent poetry here and there, its general standard of versification and the noble tone of most of it, makes it a foundation work of Scottish poetry, and one of the sources of Wallace traditions, however imperfect.

With Barbour's *Bruce*, it is the epic foundation of Scottish literature and therefore required reading for every born Scot.

Tom Scott

Chapter 1

Introduction

It is right that we should read about the good and noble deeds of our own forefathers, keeping them in mind. We are often too busy or too lazy to do this, and for too long we have honoured our English enemies and dishonoured our own heroes and benefactors. For you must understand that our enemies of English blood never yet intended any good for Scotland but have always sought to dominate the Scots by force, no matter what friendship the Scots might show them. It is well-known everywhere how they have worked, in their arrogance, to enslave Scotland forever. This has only been prevented, in the past, by the will of God and the determined resistance of our forefathers.

Among these forefathers there is one who stands out as most worthy of our respect, a man of true Scottish blood. His name was William Wallace, and it is of him that I shall tell you here. He was of honourable though not noble family. His mother was the daughter of Sir Ranald Crawford, and both he and his son (also Sir Ranald) were sheriffs of Ayr. His father was Sir Malcolm Wallace of Elderslie, and laird of other estates. Sir Malcolm was second grandson of a Wallace who served Walter, the Steward of Scotland, particularly in the matter of winning his wife, a Warren of Wales. Anybody who wants to know more about this should refer to the Stewart family records. Anyway, Sir Malcolm married the beautiful Miss Crawford, and she bore him first a son who also became Sir Malcolm Wallace, then our hero William. There was also a younger brother, John, who was murdered in London like William, who became the saviour of Scotland when treason and wicked self-seeking had lost the kingdom to the English oppressors.

When our noble king Alexander III was thrown from his horse and killed one stormy night as he rode from Dunfermline to visit Queen Yolande at Kinghorn, the realm lay desolate for three years. The great problem was who would now be king, for Alexander had left no heir. The strongest claimants to the crown were descendants of the three daughters, renowned for their beauty, of David the Earl of Huntingdon, brother of King William the Lion (1143–1214). The eldest daughter had married a Baliol, the second a Bruce, and the third a Hastings. Hastings and other lesser claimants were soon ruled out, but the choice of the Bruce and Baliol faction was so close that the law of the time made a clear decision difficult. John Baliol claimed as a great-grandson of David by the eldest daughter: Robert Bruce claimed as grandson of David by the second daughter. On such niceties hung the fate of the kingdom of Scotland, as the two factions held stubbornly to their claims. The Scots nobles sought help from learned men of law in London and Paris, but no clear ruling could be given.

To understand what follows you must know that Alexander and Edward I of England had been good friends, the kingdoms had for long been at peace, and the Scots had no reason to doubt Edward's good faith, as he was not only a great warrior (and a great rascal), but he also had a good legal mind. It seems great folly to us that the Scots nobles should turn in their plight to a man now known to be the worst enemy we ever had, but it was not so then. Edward saw his chance to grab the realm of Scotland as his own, and he took it. Having been asked for his legal opinion, he offered a political solution to each contestant: he would decide in favour of whichever one of them would do homage to him for the Crown of Scotland, thus making himself the real king of Scots. Bruce refused this treasonable way to the throne, but Baliol reluctantly accepted.

The truth is that Edward, nicknamed Longshanks, had already decided to try to conquer Scotland. He had an army already raised to conquer Gascony in France (he was a ruthless land-grabber) on the pretext that it was part of the Norman heritage of his Plantagenet family, when he was approached by the Scots to decide their dilemma. It seemed easy to take Scotland first, as it had been in his mind anyway. So Edward marched his army to Norham in Northumberland where he was met by the Scottish Privy Council. Twisting the fact that the Scottish kings had owed homage for their lands in England into their owing him homage for the kingdom of Scotland also, he now claimed to be the feudal overlord of Scotland. He was opposed by the Bishop of Glasgow, Robert Wishart, and the Privy Council, who said 'the Scottish crown has no overlord but God alone' – the truth. So Edward went behind their backs to the claimants with what result we have just seen. The Scottish crown was but a symbol of the people as a whole, and no king could dispose of it if he wanted to.

By paying homage to Edward, Baliol showed himself morally unfit to wear the Crown of Scotland. The people despised him and nicknamed him the 'toom tabard', empty coat.

Edward went south again and called a parliament, bidding Baliol attend as his representative in Scotland.

The Scottish nobles were outraged at this servile role forced on their king and put pressure on him not to attend. An abbot carried Baliol's refusal to do homage to Edward, whose rage bordered on insanity. He raised an army and came to Wark on the Northumbrian side of the Tweed, but waited there to consider before attacking Scotland.

Edward was friendly with Corspatrick, the Earl of March, and he sent to Dunbar for him and sounded him out. Edward and Corspatrick then plotted one of the most appalling atrocities in European history. The traitor went to Berwick where he was trusted as a friend and well received. Meantime, Edward moved his army up to the outskirts of the town, and after midnight, when everybody was asleep, Corspatrick let down the drawbridge of Berwick, pulled up the portcullis, and opened the gates to the English. Edward and his army took the town completely by surprise and began a massacre of men, women and children which went on for three days. It is said that the wicked tyrant only gave the order to stop when he saw a baby crying at the breast of its murdered mother. There was no Scot left alive in Berwick. Edward then left a captain in charge of Berwick and pressed on at once to Dunbar where the Scottish nobles had gathered an army of resistance.

When the English army reached Dunbar, the earls of Mar, Menteith, Atholl and Ross were in Dunbar castle, and Corspatrick and the English surprised them so that they had no time to escape and join their men before the castle was surrounded. They then slaughtered the leaderless men outside the castle, the loyal Scots outwitted by a subtler enemy.

Corspatrick was the most ruthless enemy, as traitors always are. Our fellow-Scots were slain without mercy, and the whole of that region lost. Edward and his lackey Corspatrick then rode on to Scone where they found the whole realm of Scotland defenceless.

Since times immemorial, the kings of Scots had been crowned seated on the Stone of Destiny, a block of grey basalt which the Scots had conveyed to Ireland from Spain under Gaelus who gave his name to the Gaels. Legend traced the stone back to the Holy Land and claimed that it had once been Jacob's pillow. King Fergus I brought it over from Ireland during his reign, and since circa 900AD it had remained in the safekeeping of the monks of Scone Abbey.

As Edward and his army approached Scone, the monks hid the Stone of Destiny and quickly produced a sandstone replica which they laid in its place. When Edward arrived, he deposed the puppet king John Baliol and had himself crowned whilst seated on the fake stone to fulfil the legend that whosoever was crowned on the Stone of Destiny would rule the Scots. When Edward returned to London he took the fake stone with him.

Edward also took seven score Scottish nobles and men of inheritance to London, including the young Robert Bruce, Earl of Carrick, grandson of the Bruce who claimed the Scottish throne. Edward seems to have had a special liking for young Bruce – they had more than a little in common – and made him heir to the Bruce lands in England, for which of course he owed fealty to Edward as king of England. But Edward kept a close watch on young Robert day and night, for he could see that he would make a dangerous enemy. The traitor Corspatrick was later made 'Protector' of Scotland for his treason against Scotland, but he did not hold the office long.

Meanwhile, William Wallace who was but a youth when Alexander's death brought such woe to Scotland, saw his country betrayed and occupied by the barbarous English. His father and elder brother had gone to Dunbartonshire in the early days of the troubles, and he himself had gone with his mother to her brother in Kilspindie in the Carse of Gowrie. From there Wallace was sent to school in Dundee, where he became known as an able and intelligent student. After Edward's usurpation of the Scottish crown and the brutal occupation of the country, Wallace saw many atrocities committed by the English invaders, the murder of nobles, destruction of castles, rape of the nobles' ladies, of virgins and even nuns, in barbarous sport. Like Herod, the English murdered babes at the breast. English bishops were set over Scottish sees and all other high offices, both clerical and secular, were filled by the English oppressors. They cared neither for Pope nor priest but grabbed all by right of conquest. Priests and nobles were hanged for resisting, and the Bishop of Durham was given power over Glasgow, Berwick and other Scottish sees.

All these things aroused a great anger in William Wallace, an anger which at first he had to control. He was a strong giant of a man, as great in virtue as in body, being intelligent, good-natured and upright. As Wallace developed in maturity at Gowrie, he felt the English atrocities weigh more heavily on him. He always carried side-arms for his personal defence, and he could and did use them expertly. He was not easily given to laughter, but of grave countenance even as a boy, and he spoke very little, though always good-mannered.

One day Wallace was sent to Dundee, and in a street there, finely dressed in green, a magnificent figure of a man, he was spotted by a young Englishman called Selby. Young Selby was the arrogant son of the English overlord of Dundee and he was used to gaming in that town with three or four of his friends. Taunting Scots who dared not answer back was a favourite game of his, and he approached Wallace saying, 'Hey, wait a minute, Scotsman, what are *you* doing in such finery? A hieland plaid is good enough for the likes of you, and no better weapon than a gully-knife.' So saying, he reached forward to steal Wallace's handsome dagger. Quick as a ferret Wallace seized him by the scruff of the neck and stabbed him to death before his friends could help.

Then they came at Wallace in a huddle, but he stabbed his way out and fled. He knew a house nearby where his uncle often put up for the night and he made straight for it. Once there he blurted out his news to the goodwife, seeking her help. She, hating the invaders as much as any other Scot, was quick to think up a disguise for him. She huddled him into women's clothes, knowing the district would be searched for him, put a mutch-cap on his head and set him in a dark corner at a spinning-wheel. Sure enough, it was not long before a couple of English soldiers ran in, looked hastily through the house, and ran out again, swearing at the goodwife as she wrung her hands and asked what was wrong. Wallace stayed there till darkness fell, when the goodwife led him a little-known way out of the town, avoiding the gates where the guards kept watch. He made his escape back to Gowrie, but the English took a terrible revenge on the Dundonians, setting fire to houses and burning people alive.

Wallace's mother and uncle were horrified when he told them how he had killed young Selby, fearing for his life and theirs. His mother wept, knowing her son was set on a road which must lead to his early and violent death. Wallace comforted her as best he could, but told her that he could no longer endure the insufferable hatred and arrogance of the bloody English. His uncle said little, but he was deeply worried, for he knew the English too well.

Meantime, a district court was set up in Dundee, and many Scots were arrested and charged.

Wallace Goes Fishing

The Dundee area was now dangerous for Wallace so he and his mother moved south-west disguised as pilgrims. As they travelled, Wallace had no arms except a dirk hidden under his cloak although he was in the midst of ruthless enemies after his blood. If any prying Englishman asked about their business, his mother replied that they were going to the shrine of Saint Margaret. This questionable 'saint' had been Malcolm Canmore's English queen, beloved by the English for her anglicising of the Scots court and church, but regarded as 'a sair saint' as far as Scotland was concerned. Wallace and his mother passed through Lindores and the Ochils to Dunfermline, where they stayed the night. Then they went on to Linlithgow, the wife of an English captain taking a fancy to the young giant on the way, and further on to Dunipace in Stirlingshire. Wallace had an uncle here, his father's brother, and this man, burly and kind like all the Wallaces, made them welcome to his house. William thanked him and they discussed the English oppression, the young fugitive swearing he would at least take part vengeance on the English before he was through. The older man saw too much danger and perhaps youthful folly in this, and William and his mother soon pressed on to their home-country in Elderslie, where they discovered that both William's father and brother had been killed by the invaders. Wallace's mother was very distressed and sent for her brother Sir Ranald Crawford to come and help her. He soon came, asking what he might do to help her in her terrible grief. Sir Ranald was in the feudal protection of the English Lord Percy, so she asked him to seek his protection for her also as she was tired of war and would flee no further. Her brother managed to arrange this for her, but Wallace himself would have none of it and, as his uncle was sheriff of the Ayr district, he had to leave. He said goodbye to his mother and took the road to yet another uncle, Sir Richard Wallace of Riccarton, a renowned knight. Sir Richard had been blinded in a fight with the English, but he was wise and gave Wallace good counsel, and William stayed with him from February till April.

On the 23rd of that month, it happened that Wallace went fishing on the River Irvine with bag-net and pole, taking only a young gillie with him. He made the mistake (he never made it again) of going unarmed. They fished all day and had a good catch before setting off home. Now it chanced that the Lord Percy passed that way riding with a company to the fair at Glasgow, and some of his men spotted the fishers down by the river. Five of them left the group and rode down to meet Wallace coming up from the waterside. The leading Englishman said to Wallace, 'You there, Scotchman, give us your fish – just what we need for drying and storing.' Wallace wanted to avoid trouble so he said reasonably, 'You can have half of them if you like,' and he told the gillie to hand over half of the catch. 'We'll have the lot!' said the Englishman, getting off his horse and grabbing the bag from the youth. 'You have no right to take these,' said Wallace through a set mouth, trying to keep control. 'You dare say that to me, Scotchman? I'll teach you to know your place with an Englishman,' said the other, as he ran at Wallace with drawn sword. Wallace was dismayed at being unarmed, but he struck the other such a blow on the face with his pole that it lifted him off his feet, the sword flying from his grasp, and laid him senseless. Wallace quickly grabbed the sword and killed the fallen man, stabbing him through the neck. By that time, the others were on him. One immediately fell, slashed across the neck, another had his sword hand sheared from his arm. The other two, appalled by the strength of this slashing, whirling giant, took to their heels and ran. They reached their horses, mounted as quickly as they could, and rode off after Lord Percy and his company.

Wallace turned and slew the man whose hand he had struck off. Three men dead, two escaped – and when they caught up with Lord Percy they blurted out all that had happened in a state of great fear. 'What! ONE man?' said Percy. 'Against five?' And he laughed at them and rode on saying, 'It serves you right for being such poltroons. I'll waste no time looking for one man.'

Wallace and the gillie took up their fish and gear and made for home as fast as possible. He told his uncle what had happened, and the old man was very worried about the killing of the Englishmen. 'I'm sorry to hear that,' he said, 'for if they bring this deed home to you, God help you'. 'I'll bide here no longer, uncle,' said Wallace, 'but will borrow one of these Ayrshire horses of yours.' And he left with provisions and the promise of more if they were needed.

Chapter 2

Wallace in Ayr

Young Wallace was blessed with all the virtues of manhood, chief among them his skill with arms and his loyalty to family, friends and country. The death of his father and brother weighed heavily on him and his heart burned with hatred of the English and lust for vengeance. He then rode to Auchencruive near Ayr, where he had another kinsman who made him welcome. He wanted to visit Ayr again, and one day went on foot with his squire into the town, leaving his horse in a wood nearby. Now Ayr was held by Percy and many English soldiers. They dominated the whole town by numbers and bullying arrogance, to the undoing of many a native Scot. Wallace strode confidently among them, his youth and strength proof against all fear.

Now there was one English peasant there who was a man of great strength, used to bearing very heavy loads – he could lift more than any two ordinary men. He carried a big pole with him, the kind used for carrying heavy loads slung between two men. For sport and profit this man used to offer to let any man hit him on the back with his own pole as hard as he liked for payment of one groat. When Wallace heard this offer in the market-place, you can imagine how exultant he felt at this opportunity to get something of his own back on the English. 'One groat?' said he. 'Man, I'll gie ye three.' The Englishman accepted, Wallace took the big pole, measured up to the man, and struck him such a blow that he broke his back and stretched him dead at his feet. Other Englishmen round about closed in, but Wallace, brandishing the big pole, lashed out on all sides, dashing the brains from one, breaking the neck of another, until with one mighty blow the pole itself was broken. Wallace then drew his sword and hacked his way out of the crowd, killing about half a dozen of them before he got out of town. He reached his horse in the woods then he and his waiting squire rode off under the trees. Many Englishmen tried to follow both by horse and foot, but they soon lost track of them in the deer forest.

Wallace stayed with his kinsman at Auchencruive a bit longer, but he longed to see the town of Ayr again and one market-day he set out to visit it. Now it chanced that on the same day his uncle, the Sheriff of Ayr, sent a servant into town to buy some salmon. As the man was making his purchase, along came the Lord Percy's steward, and seeing the fish just bought said, 'You there, Scotchman, where are you going with the fish?' 'To my master, the Sheriff of Ayr,' the man replied. 'By Jesus you won't,' said the steward. 'The Lord Percy will be fine pleased with these – you can get some more.' So saying he stole the fish from the man.

It so happened that Wallace had come along just in time to hear mention of the Sheriff of Ayr, and had seen the rest of the business. He went up to the Englishman and said quite reasonably, 'Look, my friend, give the Sheriff's servant back his fish and leave him alone.' The arrogant steward swore at Wallace: 'You mind your own damn business, Scotchie, or you'll be in big trouble.' So saying, he struck at Wallace with a stick he was carrying, striking him a glancing blow as he dodged under it and seized him by the collar. A second later, Wallace's knife was deep in the man's heart, and he fell dead.

There were about eighty English soldiers policing the Scots in the market square that day and a band of them ran at Wallace with drawn swords. The first to approach fell stabbed through the heart by Wallace's own sword, and others were slashed by the whirling edge. One had his leg cut off above the knee, whilst another was stabbed in the throat through chain mail. Wallace was ferocious as a lion in battle, but guards rushed at him with long spears and despite the light armour Wallace was wearing things looked very bad for him. He managed to sidle out of the square onto the sea wall but was trapped there, sheering off the heads of pikes thrust at him. Other men came running from the castle to help their comrades and Wallace decided to sell his life dearly if he had no chance of saving it. The great sword whirled and whunnered about his head, wreaking terrible vengeance on all who came into its range, till at last the mighty blade broke at the hilt. Wallace drew his dirk, but was soon borne down under the spears. Badly wounded, the captain gave orders to take him alive – they wanted to kill him slowly.

In spite of his struggles, they grasped Wallace and dragged him away by force of numbers. Thus the good Wallace, being alone and without help, was captured by the English, his great courage not enough by itself against so many. And even if his kindred had been able to afford a king's ransom, they couldn't have bought him back from the English of whose best men he alone had slain seven in the fight. They threw him into prison where he was so tortured, abused and wretchedly fed that the wonder is that he survived. His jailers fed him nothing but soused herring and water, useless to sustain such a man. 'Almighty God,' said Wallace, 'I yield my sad spirit and soul into your hands. My life cannot survive. Too few of the English have I managed to slay before my own end, but thy will be done, if I am to die in prison. O blessed Scotland, your nation stands in great peril and in need of succour, but I am helpless to do any more for you.'

O dear Wallace, once so tough and strong, now in prison cast! They kinsmen cannot buy you back with money, though ladies weep for you, the gentle and kindly ones, and your own mother, to whom you are dearer than gold. Gladly she would die for you who were ever foremost in battle.

> O saints in heaven, against his fate appeal,
> Appeal in terms conforming to His will.
> Complain of his treatment in that wretched cell,
> His torture and his pain, his anguish fell,
> And for the cause of Scotland, saints, appeal!

Why should we Scots ever trust the English? Look what suffering they have brought to our people who bow only to their rightful rulers. May God enable us yet to throw off the English yoke and deliver our country.

Wallace's sufferings in jail were now increased by an attack of enteritis which brought him to death's door. Indeed, when the jailer came to bring him to trial and death, he found him lying as if already dead. When he told his masters they gave orders that Wallace's body should be thrown on a nearby midden and left to rot. This was done.

Now it happened that the woman who had nursed Wallace as a baby heard of this and she asked permission to take the body and give it a Christian burial. The English consented reluctantly and she had the body brought to her own house without delay. Here, as she was washing it with warm water, she noticed the eyelids flicker and felt the heart move. Immediately she went to work, reviving him with warm milk; and her own daughter, who was then nursing a child of her own, fed Wallace with the milk of her own breasts. He made a quick recovery and soon they were able to make him comfortable in bed. They had to be very secretive. They gave word that he was dead and the house was set apart for a period of wake. They wept outwardly and lamented, while secretly nursing him back to health and strength.

It so happened that at this time Thomas the Rhymer was nearby visiting his friend the minister of Faille. Thomas was highly regarded by folk as a man of great learning and wisdom. He was believed to have prophesied many things long before they actually happened, things both good and ill. I can't vouch for the truth of this, for only God knows whether a battle will be lost or won. The minister's servant heard the news of Wallace's capture while shopping at the market one day, and of his death. When he returned home his master asked him what news he had heard. 'Nothing much,' he replied. 'That's funny,' the minister said, 'for wherever Scots and English gather together in one place there's usually trouble from one side or both.' 'Well,' said the man, 'you will have heard about the capture of this chap Wallace. It seems he starved to death in prison and they cast his body out on a midden. I saw it with my own eyes.' 'That calls for revenge,' said the minister, 'for he was a man of good family and a power for Scotland.'

Thomas the Rhymer, who stood listening to all this, said:

> These tidings are not good,
> If this be true, never shall I eat bread,
> For all my mind here shortly I conclude.

The man went on: 'After they cast him on a midden a woman came and asked if she could take his body away for burial and with bad grace they let her. I believe she took him to her house.' Then Thomas said:

> If that be true then I shall live no more,
> By God who maketh all things here.

The minister, seeing Thomas so upset, ordered his servant to go to the woman's house and find out the true position. The man went readily enough, and having got there, went in without knocking. He looked swiftly around as the woman came to meet him and saw a body on the table. 'Whose corpse is this?' he challenged. 'The good William Wallace,' she answered, weeping. The servant, however, did not believe her and went over to the table. The woman then fell on her knees crying, 'For the love of Mary, let it be, think no evil thoughts.' The man said, 'By the Maker of all things, if I could but see Wallace alive the secret would be safe with me though all England was after him.' She then took him to where Wallace sat, and the two men spoke together. The servant then hurried back to his master with the good news, and on hearing this Thomas prophesied: 'Truly, before he dies, many thousands shall fall in battle and he shall drive the English out of Scotland and restore her peace. Never again will Scotland know such a mighty champion.'

Don't mistake me: I know many of you will say no man equals Robert Bruce. But Wallace was in many ways his equal, in dash, skill with the sword, and even bolder in battle. Bruce of course was honoured as heir to the throne, and in that sense was unparalleled. But Wallace did in fact win Scotland from the English, and raided deep into England as well.

But to our tale. While Wallace regained his strength, the whole realm believed him dead – even his nearest kin. But once he was fit to ride again he was impatient to be up and away, so he sent his faithful old nurse, her daughter and grandchild and their servant to his own people at Elderslie, not daring to leave them to the English once the truth was known.

Wallace was without weapons, but there was an old rusty sword in a corner of the house, without a belt or buckler, but the blade still seemed strong and serviceable. 'God helps his own,' said Wallace, 'and this will have to do till I can find better – may it be soon.' Because of the English occupation he could not go at once to his uncle Sir Ranald, so he decided to go to Riccarton to seek a horse and arms.

As Wallace made his way there, he ran into three Englishmen riding to Ayr, returning from Glasgow. One of them was a fierce warrior, a certain squire called Longcastle. The other two were simple yeomen. Wallace tried to slip past them, stepping aside out of their way, but Longcastle rode up to him and said with a sneer: 'Heh, just a minute Scotty, you must be a spy or a rogue to try to slip past us like that.' Wallace replied mildly, 'Sir, I am a sick man and no danger to anybody. Just let me go on home.' 'YOU sick!' sneered Longcastle. 'You're as sturdy a warrior as ever I set eyes on. You'd better come with us till we check up on you in Ayr.' So saying he whipped out his sword, a noble brand. Wallace at once leapt into action and the old sword caught Longcastle on the side of the neck, shearing through muscle and bone. The other two came at him, but Wallace split the skull of the first down to the chops, and the last fled for his life with Wallace hard on his heels. He caught up and stabbed him to the heart with one clean thrust. He then took the dead men's horses, weapons, armour and the money they had with them, and as he rode off he thanked God for his good luck.

Wallace then sped on to Riccarton where he was met by a happy gathering of friends, among them the knight Sir Richard who had mourned for him at his supposed death. His three sons were also loyal to Wallace. Soon Wallace's uncle, Sir Ranald, having heard the glad news, arrived in Riccarton. He scarcely dared believe it until he saw his nephew face to face – at which he threw his arms round the young man in a hearty bear-hug. He could scarcely speak for emotion, his eyes welling with tears of joy. Then he said, 'Welcome home my dear nephew, my son, thank God for your deliverance from prison.' Wallace's mother and other friends also joined in the rejoicing. Robert Boyd, that man of strength and worth, would not believe the news till he too was convinced by his own eyes and people came from all over to rejoice in Riccarton.

Chapter 3

Loudon Hill and After

In glad July when the lovely flowers and fruit burgeon plentifully under the summer sun in every glen and howe, and cattle and sheep browse richly in Nature's abundance, when all birds, beasts and fishes rejoice in the providence of their almighty creator, man is surrounded by abundant food.

But not in Scotland, where for too long war had wasted and ravaged the land and the peasants laboured in vain. Food was scarce even before August and what there was, people couldn't afford to buy. But the English, having no lack of cash, had food in abundance. They filled their houses and castles with food and drink, treated the country as if it belonged to them and forced the people to do their will.

Now came news of Wallace's survival. Couriers brought it to the Lord Percy and it was readily believed after the discovery of the bodies of Longcastle and his yeomen. The English were troubled by fear of Wallace himself and their superstitious belief in the prophecy regarding him mentioned earlier. Percy said, 'It's obvious that unless this man is stopped at once he will do great deeds of mischief against us. The best thing King Edward can do is try to win him over to our side with bribes of land and wealth. There's little chance of overcoming him by force, as his amazing survival makes clear.'

Wallace for his part decided to stay no longer in Riccarton no matter what his friends or personal feelings seemed to counsel. He wanted vengeance on the English for the murder of his kindred and other fellow-Scots, and none could break his determined will.

Of Sir Richard's three sons, Adam, Richard and Simon, Adam the eldest was both brave and good-mannered, a big chap of eighteen with good sense to match his manly virtue. He was later knighted by the good King Robert and served valiantly in his campaign against the English. He now followed Wallace as squire, and they were joined by other men who could no longer bear the English yoke – Robert Boyd, who had never made obeisance to Edward; Kneland, a close kinsman of Wallace, and Edward Little, his nephew, among them. Together with their servants they rode out from Riccarton to Mauchline Muir where they stayed for a time. When friends brought them news that Fenwick, who was responsible for the deaths of Wallace's father and elder brother, was bringing tribute money from Carlisle to Percy in Ayr, Wallace took great pleasure in the news and rode towards Loudon to intercept him. As night drew on they settled in a shaw to watch the road. A loyal Scot who kept an inn nearby saw them arrive and quietly hurried to them with meat and drink, and gave them further news of the convoy, whose forerunner had already reached Ayr. The convoy itself and its strong escort was now in Avondale. Wallace gave orders that his company should stay in the shaw with the bulk of their clothes on, ready for action. Wallace himself, after his prison experience, always wore armour under his cloak, had a steel helmet under his bonnet, steel gloves and a steel collar. His face was always bare and he trusted his own mighty hands to guard it better than any visor, and thus attired, there was no man dare approach him in the heat of battle. So mighty were the works of his sword he was worth a hundred men to the Scots. As dawn broke, the Scots under Wallace moved on to Loudon Hill where they picked a place of ambush to wait for the English and sent out scouts who soon reported back that the English were fast approaching. Wallace and his men then humbly knelt and prayed to God to help them in their just cause, after which they armed themselves both morally and physically.

Wallace then addressed his men: 'My father and my brother were slain here, and so shall I be if I do not avenge them on the traitor Fenwick who even now is beginning to climb the hill.' The rising sun now lit up the terrain and as the English and their escorted baggage-train neared, Fenwick saw the Scots ahead. He told his assembled men: 'Yon is Wallace, who escaped from our prison. We shall drag him back to it through the town. I'm sure his head will please the king better than gold, lands, or any other earthly riches.' He left the baggage to the servants and took all his men forward, about two hundred of them against Wallace's fifty.

The English were confident in their numbers and their superiority in battle, and they came on fast. The Scots had made a dyke of stones which narrowed the road, and they held the field on foot. This gave the English greater confidence and they pressed on to ride the Scots down, only to find the Scots spears piercing their trampling horses even through their armour. Wallace himself ran a spear through the first man, shattering the spear-haft. He then drew his great sword and whirled into terrible action. Horses and Englishmen fell among the Scots on foot as they hacked in under belly and sword till soon the flowers were soaked with the blood of men and horses. The battle was intense, fiercely contested on both sides, attack and defence, with much courage and hardihood shown by men of both sides. Fenwick himself, a fierce and merciless warrior, well skilled and experienced in war, determined on victory and personal glory, came roaring through on his great charger glittering with armour. Wallace, who was seeking Fenwick, suddenly saw the murderer of his father and brother and became as ferocious as a lion. He surged through the battle towards him and began to rain terrible blows on him with his great two-handed sword, one of which cut the saddle-girth bringing Fenwick crashing to the ground, on the other side from Wallace, and he was slain at once by Boyd. Boyd himself was thrown to the ground and Wallace had to rush to his aid, giving him time to find his feet again, when both returned to the slaughter. Adam Wallace, the heir of Riccarton, carved through the neck of an English squire called Beaumont, but the hardy English fought bravely on. Riderless horses dashing about half-crazed made things difficult for both sides and trampled many underfoot. Many Englishmen dismounted and fought on foot like the Scots, but wherever Wallace and that terrible whirling sword of his went they were mown down like willows, and soon it was obvious they were tiring and losing heart. Wallace, Boyd, Little and Kneland all did a power of killing that day, as did many other men. The English began to flee, grabbing at horses, running for their lives, or limping wounded from the field. But most lay dead where they fell: perhaps a third escaped. The Scots helped themselves to the gear, arms, gold, horses and such left on the dead men and on the deserted field. They forced the English servants to take the baggage to Clyde's Forest, and once safely there, hanged the lot from the branches of the trees. Wallace spared no man fit for war, but he did spare the women and clerics. That night they feasted off the captured food and wine which God had delivered into their hands. They took in all two hundred baggage horses laden with flour, wine and other stuff the English had brought from Carlisle. Those of the English contingent who got away headed despondently for the Castle of Ayr and told the lord their woeful news, how much they had lost, the men killed in battle, and how the mighty Wallace had hanged all the servants.

On hearing this, Percy said: 'If that squire goes on like this he will drive us clean out of Scotland: a man so courageous in war I have never seen. We were fools to let him slip from our grasp when we had him in prison, our jailers are to blame for that. It's now almost impossible to get our provisions by the land route and we'll have to try the sea. But nothing can repair the loss of our men and their kin may curse the luck that ever brought them to Scotland.'

Now that Wallace had completely conquered and destroyed the false tyrant who murdered his father and brother and so many other good men, he divided the spoil and made provision for his followers. He also sent some to various friends nearby, and the remainder was merrily eaten before they left that place. They stayed there for about three weeks and any unlucky Englishmen who strayed near them were swiftly killed.

Wallace's fame spread far and wide, his amazing survival and astonishing deeds of arms bringing joy to the Scots and confusion to the English. Percy rode to Glasgow to seek advice from his seasoned peers there. Their assembled forces ran to some ten thousand but no leader could be found who was able and willing to lead them against Wallace. Percy was at a loss and asked his superiors' advice. Sir Aylmer de Valance, a mighty and false traitor living in Bothwell, spoke up: 'My lord, here is my advice and unless you take it God help you. You must seek a truce with Wallace at once and play for time till we can inform the King himself.' Percy replied, 'I can't see Wallace making any truce with us. He is a ferocious chief and thinks the only good Englishman is a dead one – he slays without the least compunction.' Sir Aylmer said, 'All the same it is imperative to try, and we will deal with Wallace later. I know he is very loyal to his kinsmen, honour and nobility being habitual with him.

We might get at him through his uncle, Sir Ranald: try persuading him to get Wallace to make a truce, and if he won't, seize his lands.'

Sir Ranald was brought before them and they made it clear to him that he should persuade Wallace to make peace or else he would be sent to London. Sir Ranald said: 'My lords, you know as well as I do that nothing I say will make the least difference to Wallace. You slew his dearest kin, you cast him out for dead after abusing him in jail, and now that he is free and in arms, though you were to slay me on the spot, you would not stop him – on the contrary.' Sir Aylmer replied: 'Once the King hears the news these lords have sent him, this matter will be ended for ever, whatever you or Wallace do. But if Wallace could be won over to Edward for land or gold and become his liegeman in Scotland, Edward would give him power over the whole country.'

Hearing this the other lords protested, saying: 'You are proposing for Wallace more power and glory than becomes his humble rank, and the King will never hear of it. He seeks to rule by conquest, not by currying favour, and he would be furious at such a suggestion, whatever Wallace's undoubted qualities.' But Lord Percy went on trying to persuade Sir Ranald: 'You are Sheriff of Ayr, Sir Ranald, and I for my part will bind myself to be responsible for seeing that every Englishman shall keep the peace nor seek to take Wallace or any other Scot, unless provoked.' Sir Ranald saw that he could not withstand them. Percy was a true knight, sincere in peace, terrible in war, and of great influence. He agreed therefore to seek out Wallace and he set off for the great forest of Clyde. There he soon found his nephew, arriving just at dinner-time. He was well received, though Wallace was surprised to see him and wondered what he wanted. He gave him generous hospitality and such food and wine as might have come from King Edward himself: they had plenty of venison and all sorts of meats and provender. It was only when the dinner was over that Sir Ranald told Wallace how he had been coerced into proposing a truce with the English to Wallace. He went on to point out that if Wallace failed to agree, he would bring disaster on his kinsmen.

Wallace was against any truce, but he consulted his companions at the table. Sir Robert Boyd was of the opinion that it might be best to make a temporary truce to save Sir Ranald's life and a number of other important men were of the same opinion. Wallace accepted their suggestion and authorised his uncle to negotiate a ten-month truce with the English. They took their farewells of each other in friendship, invoking St John the Beloved to preserve them all till they met again. The band broke up, most of the chief men going home: but Wallace went with his uncle Sir Ranald to stay with him in Crosby.

This dubious peace was signed in the pleasant month of August, but Mars, the god of battle, enraged and untameable, and the goddess Juno, went on stirring up strife, as did Venus the goddess of love and beauty, Mars's camp-follower and mistress, and lugubrious old Saturn. They found fertile soil for their sowing wherever there were Scots and English.

Wallace soon tired of inaction at Crosby and longed to be once again in arms, and one day when Sir Ranald was away, Wallace took fifteen men and rode for the town of Ayr. He kept his face well-covered in hope he would not be recognised by any of the enemy he might run into. His men were also kept well muffled up against recognition.

It happened that on the way to Ayr they ran into an Englishman who was practising skirmishing techniques, his shield on his arm. Wallace and his men stood and watched. When the man saw them, he joked, 'Well, Scotty, have you the guts to try a cut at me?' Wallace replied, 'Yes, if you feel like it.' 'Any time,' said the man. 'Lay on as hard as you like.' Wallace took his sword and struck at the man's head and though the man shielded himself with great skill the sword sheared through shield, shield-arm and skull, splitting him down to the chin. Great was the hullabaloo among the women standing round. Armed men came running as if from nowhere and soon Wallace and his fifteen companions were beset by many times their own number. Wallace's mighty figure whirled his five-foot two-handed sword with such ferocity and skill that any who came within range paid with his life, and his men were inspired to deeds beyond their own unaided custom. Scotland lost many enemies that day. But as new forces kept arriving from the castle Wallace covered his men as they all retreated, and once clear they rode full-pelt for Laglyne wood. The English, with thirty dead on the field, dared not follow into the wood and hastened back to the town, cursing the truce they had entered into.

Lord Percy was furious when he heard the news, his mind having been temporarily lulled by the truce. Three of his own kin were among the dead, and when he heard the English had brought it on themselves, being the first to attack – for the killing of the warrior had been fair play – he was doubly aggrieved. The Scots of course did not know this. Percy then sent to Sir Ranald, ordering him to keep Wallace away from the market, town or fair where inevitably he would run into English soldiers. But though the English knew it was Wallace who had wrought such havoc among them, they still held to the truce – too much was at stake. When Wallace got home from Laglyne, Sir Ranald showed him the letter from Lord Percy, and begged Wallace to honour the truce, not to stray, and to kill no more Englishmen meantime. Wallace could not agree to this plea but promised to make no more trouble while actually staying with his uncle, intimating that he would soon let him know when he would leave. This satisfied his uncle, and after a few days Wallace took his leave. No matter how well he was treated by his uncle, he could not forget that his beloved country was overrun by the English enemy.

Chapter 4

Wallace in the Lennox

In the douce month of September when the height of
summer is past and the harvest of grain and fruit is
ripening, God's blessing on mankind, the leaves have lost
their summer brightness and the year declines towards
the winter solstice as the season changes: in this month
the English lords held a great council in Glasgow to make
rules and laws to govern Scotland. All the stooge sheriffs
were ordered to attend, Sir Ranald Crawford among them
as sheriff of his native Ayr. He took with him his beloved
nephew William Wallace, as the book bears witness,
being unwilling to let him out of his sight for any length
of time. They fully armed themselves and rode off,
Wallace and two of his stout warriors leading the way.
Suddenly, at Hazeldean, they saw Lord Percy's provision
horse richly laden but so exhausted it could go no further.
Five men escorted it, two on foot and three on horseback,
and seeing Sir Ranald's provision horse, the leader said,
'Whose provisions are these?' The boy in charge of Sir
Ranald's provision horse said, 'My lord's, the Sheriff of
Ayr.' 'Well in that case we'd better take it along with us,
for our master is superior to yours and has greater need.'
They then tried to take over the loaded horse. Wallace,
seeing this robbery but unwilling to get involved in more
trouble at present, tried to reason with them, reminding
them of the truce. The English bully rounded on him

angrily and used the Scotsmen's horse to take the load from their own exhausted animal. Wallace controlled his rage with difficulty but contented himself for the time being with telling his uncle what had happened. Sir Ranald shrugged it off, saying: 'Well, better a horse and gear than men's lives.' Wallace replied, 'As God is my witness I shall be avenged for this villainy, and neither truce nor feeling for you shall prevent me. If you choose to forfeit your rights out of cowardice I hereby renounce my allegiance to you, and you yourself will get nothing but death out of it.' And he left Sir Ranald in anger. Sir Ranald, being shrewd, considered his position and decided to stay all night at the Mearns so that no blame would attach to him if Wallace should slay any of the English, and the case come to trial. But he was sorry to lose Wallace's respect and feared for his nephew's rash and futile behaviour, as it seemed to him.

Wallace rode on with his two yeomen and chased after the English who had stolen the provision horse, overtaking them at Cathcart. The five men recognised him and came to meet him as he slid from his horse and drew the great sword from its scabbard on his shoulder. The leader was first to meet him, and his head was sliced from his shoulders at one stroke of that mighty blade. The next was struck in the face and fell dead, and a third followed him. The other two were already slain by the two yeomen, and Wallace commandeered the spoil, gear, horses, gold, silver, jewels, and rode off. As they crossed a wooden bridge over the Clyde and night drew in, Wallace determined to acquire more men.

Glasgow was too dangerous for Wallace to stay near, so he decided to make for the Lennox. They spent the night there with loyal Scots friends in a hostel. Next day the English council met in Glasgow only to hear Percy's news of how the Scots had slain his servants and stolen his gear and jewels. They discussed the terrible events and had no difficulty in recognising the work of Wallace. They vented much of their rage on poor Sir Ranald who was in a vulnerable position as Sheriff. But it was obvious to the more intelligent of the English that he could not have known anything about the matter. Nevertheless, some tried to bring a charge of complicity against him, but Sir Ranald had little difficulty in convincing the judge that he was ignorant of the whole business and his nephew's whereabouts.

Meanwhile, Wallace, with none but God as his guide, wandered abroad for four days before hearing news of the council, which had issued orders that he was to be hunted down and given no rest from pursuit, and had put Sir Ranald on oath for his life to give Wallace no help or succour. The little band had split up for the time being, though Boyd, Kneland and others longed to be with their beloved chief again. Edward Little, home in Annandale, heard nothing of the new statute, nor did Adam Wallace in Riccarton and none of them knew where to find Wallace.

Wallace decided it would be a good thing to head north for a time and sound out the chiefs there. He decided that Earl Malcolm of Lennox, who had never sworn fealty to Edward, would be a good man to start with and sought him out at once. That loyal noble was delighted to meet the great freedom fighter and made him most welcome in the Lennox, inviting him to take command of his own household and be chieftain over the Lennox men. Wallace was honoured, but excused himself on the ground that he must carry on the struggle for Scotland as and where he could, and must press further north.

Stephen of Ireland, being then in the Lennox, was appointed by the Earl to go with Wallace, as were certain men of Argyll. Others came to join him. Wallace had to take them all on trust as they were strangers to him, welcoming them, but keeping an eye on them all the same, for fear of a possible traitor. Some of these men came from Ireland where they had run foul of one MacFadyean, a commoner who pretended to be born of the English aristocracy, a traitor and lackey of the English king.

Among these men was one called Fawdoun, a man of dour and saturnine face, never cheerful but always of serious, even fearful nature. Wallace welcomed all who came to him and who, in front of Earl Malcolm, promised loyalty to Wallace as captain and leader. His own friends from home, Gray and Kerlie, had stuck with him ever since Loudon Hill and, trusting them fully, Wallace made them his lieutenants. The good earl wanted to load presents on Wallace but that worthy man politely refused to take anything but necessities. He was ever generous to those in need, but never grasping for himself. He had no property or wealth, no false pride, but had many virtues; endurance, wisdom and liberality among them. In fact, Wallace was a mirror of all that is best in a man: honour, reverence, courage, ability and incorruptible integrity. Any gold fairly won from the enemy was shared out generously. This was the young man who led some sixty men out of the Lennox.

Wallace and his company camped for a time in a glen above Leckie where there was a castle held by the English. This small castle or peel of Gargunnock, Wallace intended to win back. It was well manned and had lots of food and other provisions in it, and it was surrounded by a moat. Wallace reconnoitred, learning all he could about the place and its Captain, an Englishman called Thirlwall, through his spies.

On a certain night he sent two of his spies to the castle itself and they reported that the man on watch seemed fast asleep and that the drawbridge was down with workers moving freely out and in. Wallace, who did not want to take any risks on this venture, judged the time ripe for the attempt. He and his men quickly armed themselves, quietly made their way to the keep and simply walked in unchallenged. Once inside they found themselves faced by a huge door, barred and padlocked, clearly guarding gear and provisions. Some of his men tried to force the door, but without success till Wallace, annoyed at the waste of time, hurled his mighty bulk at it, not only bursting the bar out of the wall it was socketed in but tearing some three feet of wall out with it. His men were amazed at this giant feat of strength. There was a gate inside, and this Wallace also burst open, this time with a mighty kick. The men in the peel were now thoroughly alarmed and jumped from their beds grabbing up arms. The watchman struck at Wallace with a huge iron staff, but Wallace closed with him, wrested the thing from his grip, dashed out his brains with it and flung him into the moat. The garrison now came racing up, led by Thirlwall. Wallace met him with the same great staff and smashed his skull with it. Meanwhile, Wallace's men fell on the garrison and soon slew the lot – Wallace ordered none were to be spared. There were twenty-two in all. The women and children were spared, but were shut up in a chamber so that it would be some time before they could raise the alarm outside, for Wallace intended to stay in the peel for a while. They stayed in fact for four days, feasting well, and gathering all the spoil they could. Having spoiled the place, they set out one night for a nearby wood, having freed the women and children, who had been in no way molested by the Scots.

Wallace did not wish to stay long in the area and decided to cross the River Forth. They made their way across the firm turf on foot, resting the few horses they had, led by Stephen of Ireland, in the direction of Kincardine. They rested in a wood by the banks of the Teith. There were some wild animals about and Wallace set out hunting, managing to kill a big deer, which was promptly dressed and roasted back at the camp. Washed down with wine they brought from the peel it made a feast for heroes.

Wallace gave the big iron staff he had taken from the watchman to Kerlie to keep for him, and they quietly forded the Teith into Strathearn unnoticed. Here and there on the journey scouts warned Wallace of any Englishry nearby and these were mercilessly slain by the Scots with no regard for rank or station. Some were slain by stealth, others ambushed: throats were cut, all valuables taken, and the bodies hidden. At Blackford, where they intended crossing, they were mistaken for Englishmen by a squire and his four companions who all rode up in a friendly manner, only to be slain by the Scots, stripped of their gear and thrown into the river Earn. Wallace and his men then crossed over and made their way northward to Methven Wood where they stayed the night. At dawn, Wallace was impressed by the abundance of game in the area, not to mention cattle and sheep. 'This is fine country for soldiers,' said Wallace, 'who too often have to scrape along on meagre rations. Here there is plenty, and who would jib at that?' But of course throughout his campaigns Wallace and his men cared little for nicety of diet or conditions: they took whatever came, like heroes, good and ill.

His Mistress in Perth Betrays Him

After staying awhile in that happy place Wallace tired of his comfortable inaction and decided he would like to take a look at the town of St Johnston, as Perth was then called. He had heard of the English mayor there, and taking seven men with him, set out, leaving Stephen of Ireland in his place. He promised to be back in one week. On arrival, he sought out the mayor, giving his name as William Malcolmson – partly true, for his father was

Malcolm Wallace. The mayor was a bit suspicious of these stalwart Scots, but the truce still held and he therefore had to treat them hospitably. When he heard that they came from Ettrick forest he began to ask them about the terrible stories he had heard of William Wallace who, in contempt of the truce seemed to be terrorising the King's men there; a ruthless murderer.

'Yes, indeed, I have heard of him,' said Wallace, 'but there's nothing I can tell you about him.'

Wallace set about getting lodging for himself and his men and kept it well guarded. Kerlie did the catering providing plenty of good plain fare. They spent carefully what they had, cultivating Scots at drinking places and avoiding the English as much as possible. Thus Wallace got to know a good deal about the town, who the chief men were – Sir James Butler and his son John, and Sir Gerrard Heron. Wallace also took a look at the women of the town, and was much taken by a rosy-cheeked blonde who lived in South Street. They soon came to an understanding and Wallace spent happy times with her. Lying by her side he often thought about how to free Perth from the insufferable English, but decided his army was too small: and to set fire to it would only hurt friend as well as foe. The gates were close guarded, the moat deep, and some of his men could not swim. He decided to abandon the idea for the present.

Wallace was then on the point of leaving St Johnston when one of his own men brought him information that Sir James Butler would be riding to his strong castle of Kincleven at a certain time. Wallace and his men set off back to Methven wood where the rest of his men were delighted to see him. He found them in excellent spirits and quickly gathered them together. Then they made for Kincleven castle, and in a den close by they laid an ambush for Sir James. Soon three scouts of the main English party rode along and were allowed past: Wallace did not want to alarm the castle, especially as his force was small in numbers, though large in spirit.

Soon the main body of Sir James's court came riding along, some ninety of them in all, both men and horses well armoured, real warriors. Wallace thanked God their number was no greater, and sallied out upon them. The English were surprised and incredulous that this little band dared to attack them. Their surprise turned to rage, and at once they got into battle order, couched their spears and made to ride down the insolent Scots. Wallace and his men had the advantage of preparation and tore into them with deadly effect, many Englishmen being slain at the first onset. Wallace himself transfixed one with his spear, the shaft of which was shattered by the impact. He then drew his great sword, dismounted and hammered the English with it afoot. The Scots stabbed at the horses, throwing the riders and setting wild chargers trampling down their own riders. Butler himself dismounted and stood his ground among many of his men, fine soldiers all. Many a mighty deed of arms was done that day. Many Scots also fell, which infuriated Wallace, who pressed steadily on towards Butler, a man of great courage. At last Wallace broke through to Butler and his terrible stroke caught that knight on the head, shearing through steel helmet and bone into the brain. The fight was over and the rest of the English retreated as best they could. Many of the Scots were left dead on that field, but Stephen of Ireland and Kerlie did fierce work on the now fleeing English, only about thirty of whom escaped with their lives. They knew of no place of safety but the castle and made for it pell-mell, the Scots in pursuit. Only a few soldiers defended the place, and, seeing the fleeing figures, priests and women high on the walls guessed the truth and wails of grief and fear went up from them. The drawbridge was let down for the escapers and Wallace was so hard on their heels that he too got across and held the gate till his men got through. All the English in the castle, both defenders and fugitives, were put to the sword. The priests, women and children were spared, but confined for the time being. Wallace then had the drawbridge drawn up and the gate bolted. The dead bodies were hidden, except for a few Scots who were properly buried. They stayed a week in the castle eating up the edible spoil, though much of it they transferred to Shortwood Shaw along with gold, silver, furnishings and other valuable gear. The English women and children were then set free, and having laden themselves with all that was transportable from the castle, they then set fire to it. All the iron fittings were hurled into the moat, and the bridge was destroyed.

They then made good speed to Shortwood Shaw where they had a stronghold already well supplied, as we have seen. The smoke and flames from Kincleven attracted the peasantry for miles around, but when they came to the castle they found nothing but stones left standing. Lady Butler reached Perth where she told her terrible story to her son and Sir Gerrard, his superior. They realised that only Wallace could have been responsible for this outrage, and that he must have been the Malcolmson recently in Perth – spying. Orders were given to arm a troop of horse to seek out the outrageous Wallace, and about a thousand men, fully armed, five companies in all, set out for the Shortwood Shaw, surrounding it with stalwart warriors. A sixth company entered the wood to try to flush the Scots from cover.

When Wallace realised his peril he drew his men into the fortified encampment, rough and ready it was, but allowing both cover and easy exit, ready to face assault. John Butler, keen to avenge his father's death, led the two hundred men of this company, and they soon came up to Wallace's stronghold, which had a steep cliff behind it guarding their backs. Wallace had only seven archers outnumbered twenty to one against the English archers, who were covered by as many English spearmen. Wallace himself had a bow which only he could bend, and deadly work he did with it that day. But the English arrows also took their toll of the Scots, and Wallace had to try to keep his men on the move to avoid them. Occasional sallies with the sword cut swathes in the front ranks of the English bowmen. One of these sought Wallace himself and, getting a sight of him, loosed an arrow that took him sidewise under the chin, in the loose flesh of the throat – his steel collar had somewhat deflected the blow. Wallace at once dashed out on this archer and sliced off his head with a single blow of his great sword, no friend to the English.

Wallace had now used up all his arrows, while the English had an endless supply. To add to this desperate peril, William Lorn now appeared with some three hundred armed men from Gowrie – Sir John Butler had been his uncle. Soon the Scots were under intolerable pressure in their makeshift fort and Wallace gave orders that every man should prepare to sell his life dearly.

Lorn and his men, having studied the position, came in at the little band from one side, John Butler from the other, while Sir Gerrard himself commanded the force outside the wood. Wallace, in urgent need of reinforcements, had only about fifty men left to meet appalling odds. He himself did heroic work with his great two-handed sword, which he could use with only one hand, hacking down the English foe with startling speed: no armour was proof against his mighty stroke. But mightily as they fought, the Scots position was untenable and they broke out of their stronghold and fell back to a denser part of the wood where the very vegetation hampered the enemy. As his men fell dead or wounded around him, Wallace saw John Butler in the forefront of the foes and went for him like a whirlwind. Butler shielded himself behind the branch of a tree and as Wallace struck a ferocious blow at him the sword clove through the branch felling Butler with it. Before Wallace could finish the job, Butler's men rushed to his aid and some held Wallace while others dragged off their master. This was seen by Lorn who also rushed to the scene where Wallace, baulked of one enemy leader turned his full fury on him. A mighty blow struck Lorn on the gorget and sheared through steel and bone, severing the neck. Wallace fought back to the dense copse as the cry went up among the enemy that Lorn was dead. This news made Sir Gerrard leave his position outside the wood and hasten into the centre, thus leaving the way clear for Wallace and his remaining men to make their escape to the north, thanking God as they went. They managed to get to Cargill wood by nightfall. The English, who had been given the slip, thought the Scots must still be hiding somewhere in Shortwood Shaw and went on searching there till they realised they sought in vain – the prey had escaped. They also searched for the treasure Wallace had taken but found nothing at all, with the exception of one horse. It was a much vexed and frustrated troop that made its way back to Perth. Next night the Scots sent a party stealthily back to Shortwood and recovered all the goods and loot they had hidden there, and the whole party pressed on to Methven wood, where they stayed a couple of days, then went on to Elcho Park.

Wallace had not forgotten his woman-friend in Perth and, feeling the urge to visit her, disguised himself as a priest and set out. She was delighted to see him but much afraid for his safety, and her own if they were caught. He stayed with her, love-making all afternoon and slipped away again at nightfall, promising to come back in a few days. But as he left the house he was recognised by one of the enemy and he took the news at once to Sir Gerrard and Sir John Butler. Knowing they had little chance by that time of following Wallace, these gentlemen ordered their men to go and arrest the woman. When she was brought into their custody they accused her of harbouring the notorious outlaw William Wallace. She denied any knowledge of him. The noble Butler then said, 'You're lying, we know without doubt it was Wallace and if you don't help us we'll burn you at the stake. On the other hand, if you do help us we'll make you a fine lady with a real knight for a lover.' To prove it, he gave her some gold and silver. The women, who had a hard enough life of it and knew Wallace was not interested in her as a wife, was tempted, and they played on her weakness. She told them when Wallace was due to come and see her again, and they were overjoyed, wanting nothing more in this world than to take Wallace alive. So they laid a trap for Wallace at each gate of the town. Wallace, in a different disguise, nevertheless managed to slip past them and got to the woman's house undisturbed. There she received him as usual and they went to bed at once. In his arms she knew such bliss that a strong love was born for him, she longed for him to stay with her all night, forever. The temptations that had led her to betray him were swallowed up in her love and fear for his life, her hardness of heart melted, and she began to sob in his arms, and the more he tried, puzzled, to comfort her, asking what distressed her so, the more uncontrollably she sobbed, and the truth came out. 'Unhappy day that ever I was born,' she moaned, 'for I have betrayed the dearest man alive! O how could I be so weak and do so vile a deed. Cursed be the mind that brought me to such wickedness and folly. O Will!' Wallace embraced and soothed her, saying, 'Dear lass, what is all this about, what is distressing you – is it my fault?' 'Not you,' she sobbed, 'O Will, I have betrayed you to the English who threatened and tempted me with promise of wealth and status. I should have gone gladly to their fires rather than betray my love – would that I had burned for you.' And she told him the whole story through her sobs.

Wallace at first felt cold hate in his guts, then anger at the way she had been treated. He couldn't blame the girl and tried to comfort her. But he knew he was in the deadliest danger and could see no way out. Now this woman was very tall and handsome, a woman fit to walk with such a man. In the headwear of the time she would have seemed almost as tall to the casual eye. Wallace hit upon a desperate plan of escape. He borrowed a long gown and cloak from her, pulled a cap well down to his scalp, hid his sword under the cloak, muffled the cloak well up about his face and slipped out, as bent as he could, trying to make himself look smaller. He made his way to the south gate, took stock of the group of men there waiting for him, and slunk up as if afraid to be seen. He whispered in as near her voice as he could manage, 'Quick, Wallace is about to leave my house.' The men ran off toward the house where he had left the girl bound and gagged on the bed to help her escape the wrath of the English. The way clear, he slipped through the gate unhindered and out into the night. He soon straightened up in his outlandish clothes and two approaching soldiers saw him. 'Some woman that,' said one. 'Let's have a look at this giant girl.' And they ran after him. Wallace, hearing the feet, turned to see only two men and waited for them. As the first came up he suddenly flashed his sword and struck him dead. The other turned and ran but Wallace soon caught and killed him too.

Once clear, he quickly rid himself of the female garb and hastened back to his men who were delighted to see him return safely. The English soldiers found the girl tied up on the bed, cut her free, and she blurted out that Wallace had learned of her betrayal, tied her up, stolen her clothes, and was making off to the west, she thought. They dashed off in pursuit at once leaving the girl to make her escape, though where she fled to history does not tell.

Chapter 5

Wallace Slays Fawdoun

November had now set in, the dark wintry season of short days and long nights, adding to the difficulties of outlaws forced to live in discomfort in wild inaccessible country. And when men have to live through long dark nights oppressed by cold and lack of comforts of home and entertainment, their thoughts also tend to be dark and oppressive, gloomy and chill. Such thoughts weighed on William Wallace as he watched the sun go down one night and spies brought word that a party of English soldiers were on their way to seek him out in the wood where he was thus imprisoned. Some six hundred English soldiers were constantly searching for him, but this party was about a hundred. They had with them a bloodhound, more dangerous and efficient than another score of men. This hound had been bred in Gilsland and trained in Eskdale and Liddesdale. When she scented blood, it was said, nothing could outwit her. The English were sure Wallace was as good as taken.

Subsequently, the English soldiers split up into several smaller groups led by Sir John Butler. Sir Gerald Heron stayed outside the wood with the main force of about three hundred men. The alarmed Scots reconnoitred the edges of the wood for an escape exit, but wherever they looked they found soldiers waiting – the wood was surrounded. Soon the hound led her masters to where the Scots hid and they were forced to sally out in hot attack on the English, outnumbered more than two to one, not counting the English outside the wood. So bravely they fought, Wallace as ever chief among them, that they managed to carve a way through the enemy to the banks of the River Tay: but as some of the men could not swim, Wallace, who would not leave them to their fate, made a stand on a raised copse which gave them some advantage in self-defence against the English. Butler pressed hard on them with his men and a fierce struggle to the death ensued, neither side sparing steel or man. Young Wallace, alarmed to see his men wounded and killed about him, fought like a madman, seeking out Butler himself. In this he failed, but so ferocious was his attack that Butler, having come within an inch of death from that mighty sword, gave way and withdrew his men. Kerlie and Stephen of Ireland bravely distinguished themselves that day, which cost the English some sixty men. Wallace and his men managed to make their escape as Butler fell back, but the English and their bloodhound were soon in pursuit as he made for Gask Wood.

In the speed of this escape, Fawdoun began to fall behind, saying he was exhausted and couldn't go on. Wallace urged him on, being very dubious of the man and his motives. He did not believe that Fawdoun was as tired as he made out, and had long suspected him of being a traitor who now wanted to desert to the English. After many attempts to speed him up Wallace lost his temper with him, denounced him as a traitor and struck off his head. Fawdoun was no weakling but a man of great strength and stamina, not one to tire so easily, but nobody ever trusted him. Opinions differ about Wallace's wisdom in this deed, but there are two ways to look at it: if Fawdoun was a traitor, it was right to kill him, and if he was not it was better to kill him than let him fall into the hands of the English torturers. Anyway, the result was to hold up the hound for a few precious minutes while the Scots escaped to a stronghold where they could make another stand.

Two of Wallace's most trusted and valiant warriors, Stephen of Ireland and Kerlie, were left behind near Fawdoun's body to see what happened when the English discovered it. The dog seemed to think its work was now done, and it stayed excitedly yelping beside the dead body. The English began to withdraw, leaving Heron with a few men staring broodily down at Fawdoun. Taking a chance, Kerlie sauntered up beside Heron as if he were one of his own men and without warning suddenly drove his dagger up into his throat, through the mouth and into the brain, speeding off at once into the woods. Stephen, in the trees, also made his escape as the English gathered round their fallen leader. Butler was soon told the news, and came to weep over the body of Heron. Then he ordered several of the men to take his body back to Perth, while he and the rest of his men carried on in pursuit of Wallace as best they could in the darkness.

Wallace and the dozen or so men left with him, headed for Gask Hall. Stephen and Kerlie had still not caught up with him, and Wallace was a bit anxious for their safety. A fire was made in the Hall, but they had no food, so they stole a couple of sheep from a nearby fold. As these were being prepared for roasting, a blaring of horns was heard not far off, and Wallace sent two men out to investigate. They did not come back, so another two were sent. The blaring still went on, and the second pair didn't return either. Wallace became very angry and sent all his men out to see what was going on. Left alone, it seemed to him the noise got even louder, and none of the men returned. Wallace, now beside himself with anger, seized his great two-handed sword, convinced that the enemy had killed them all, and he prepared to sell his own life at the highest price. He ran outside – and froze like a statue at what he saw, for surely no man had ever seen, drunk or sober, such a sight. There before him stood Fawdoun, headless, but carrying his head in his hands. As the apparition moved slowly and menacingly towards him, Wallace unfroze enough to make the sign of the cross, but still the thing came on. When it was near enough it took the head by the hair in one hand and struck at Wallace, missed, then threw it at him. Wallace shivered all over with fear of the supernatural, the hair rising on his neck and scalp. He backed away from the ghost, then turned and ran back into the house, right to a shuttered casement there, smashed the shutters with his mighty bulk and leapt out into the night. He must have fallen quite a few feet but miraculously broke no bones, picked himself up and ran on in panic up the bank of the burn, and as he ran he looked over his shoulder and it seemed to him that the hall blazed into flames and the ghost chased after him with a huge blazing rafter.

Gradually Wallace's terror subsided; he seemed to have outdistanced his pursuer, and his pace fell to a quick walk. What had happened to his men? Had they too fallen into the power of the devil? In torment of spirit he wandered on, scarcely aware of where he was or was going, his heart pounding. At last he got a grip of himself, he who feared nothing on earth but feared the unearthly. Why should God thus torment him? Had he done great wrong in killing Fawdoun? Was God punishing him for that – and if so, why his wretched men? Were they all dead and if so, by English hands or some supernatural power? As he wandered absorbedly up the river, sometimes talking to himself, sometimes groaning, he was spotted by Sir John Butler who was watching the ford with his men. Not recognising his enemy in this rambling wanderer, Butler rode across to question him. 'Who goes there?' he called as he approached. 'Who are you and what are you doing?' The sight and sound of human flesh and blood brought Wallace to his senses. 'I am a good man and true,' he called back, 'though abroad so late. I'm on my way from Doune to my Lord Stewart.'

'You are a liar,' Butler replied, 'and I have no doubt you are one of Wallace's band of rascals and I mean to get the truth out of you.' So saying he rode up and swung down from his horse, sword in hand. He had scarcely got one foot on the ground before the great two-handed sword caught him above the knee and cut the leg off him, and as he fell, a second stroke did as much for his head. Wallace grabbed the horse as the English streamed across the ford towards him and swung into the saddle. The foremost man came at him with a spear but Wallace struck the thing in two and made off. The English caught up with him as he tried to cross a ford further up, but any who came within range of that mighty sword rued the day – or rued no more. Once across, Wallace galloped across the moor with the English hard at his heels. He managed to evade them for a time but, his horse tiring, he dismounted and walked it for about a mile, when the English caught sight of him again and renewed the chase. A small number had got detached from the main body and as they began to gain on him Wallace rode up on a knoll and turned to make a stand. After he had slain a few of them the others fell back and made off. The horse was tired out, so again Wallace tried walking it, but it was completely exhausted and he slew it rather than leave it there.

He soon found himself in sight of the Forth near Stirling. There was a convenient wooden bridge there but Wallace knew it would be guarded by English soldiers. Tired and hungry as he was, not even he could have fought his way across. He therefore decided to make for Cambuskenneth and risk the dangerous swim across the strong, icy current. He made a bundle of his gear and, praying to God for succour, he launched into the freezing water and swam boldly for the far side. Despite the cold, which numbed even his giant strength, he made it to the other side and quickly dressed and re-armed himself.

Wallace now pressed on to the Torwood where he had an old friend, a certain widow who had helped him in the past. He arrived just at daybreak and, not wanting to alarm her too much, tapped at the window and called to her in the name of friendship. He hoped she would rtecognize his voice, but at first it was a stranger who answered. Wallace refused to give his name but asked for the guidwife. When she came, she recognized the voice at once and cried out with pleasure, thanking God he was safe and well. But where were his men?

'Alas,' said Wallace, 'I haven't a single one just now.' He told her he was famished and in need of food, and that he feared all his men were dead. Once he had been fed, Wallace told of his latest adventure with the English. A woman companion of the widow agreed to go back to Gask Hall and try to find out what she could, particularly whether any of the men had survived. A young man went along with her, and they set out at once. Being exhausted, Wallace wanted somewhere to sleep but was afraid to stay in the house, so he chose a spot on the edge of the wood and there, attended by two of the widow's three sons, he soon fell asleep. Meanwhile, the widow sent her third son to Dunipace, where Wallace's uncle was priest, to tell him of the situation. The uncle came at once, and was led to the place where Wallace slept, approaching quietly. He looked down on the sleeping giant and muttered to himself, 'What a scene: here is the man who by sheer merit has halted the might of England so down on his luck that even a determined woman could slay him as he sleeps.' In a trice Wallace was on his feet, sword in hand, saying, 'You lie, you treacherous priest and I could cope with any ten of you. Only yesterday I faced far greater odds than sixty of you could make.' At this, his uncle told him who he was, and they rejoiced together. Wallace told him about his recent trials, his fights, the weird business of Fawdoun's head and the fire at the hall, the icy swim – never had he suffered so much. But the loss of all his men was the hardest of all to bear. His uncle then advised him to give up the unequal struggle, make his peace with King Edward, who would almost certainly give him a title, lands and power.

'Let me hear no more such talk,' said Wallace. 'You only add to my troubles. The only gift I want is to see the English die under my sword – that is land and gold to me. I tell you this, I will either rid Scotland of the bloody English or die in the attempt.'

Even as he spoke one of the widow's sons came up with two stalwart men – Kerlie and the good Stephen of Ireland. Tears of happiness sprang from the eyes of the three warriors as they clasped each other and capered about for sheer delight in life and reunion. Then they fell on their knees in the grass and gave thanks to the Queen of Heaven for their good luck. Wallace told them his adventures and they told him theirs, and of the death of Sir Gerrard, how they had been ferried across the river and met up with the friends of Wallace who brought them to him. Wallace's uncle got ample provisions together for them and they spent the night safely in the Torwood. As for Gask Hall, the woman told him it was still standing quite unharmed, though all his men had disappeared and she found out nothing about them. This saddened Wallace of course, but the widow told her two older sons to go with Wallace and serve him: the youngest was too young and stayed with her. She also gave them money, and Wallace's uncle found them horses, though he shook his head over his nephew's determination.

Wallace made all possible speed to Dundaff moor, where he intended to visit the good Sir John the Graham, an ageing knight who, though he had made peace with the English for the sake of a quiet life, had no love for them and grudged them every penny of tribute he had to pay them. The Graham had a son, noted for valour and ferocity in battle. This young John Graham had been knighted by the late king Alexander, and a noble, intelligent warrior he was. The old knight was not able to join Wallace in the rigours of a guerilla war but he made his son swear loyalty and service to Wallace and his cause over a broad shield, and Wallace to him, while they both should live. Wallace stayed there three nights in comparative safety and thus managed to get some much-needed rest. On the fourth day he decided it was time to move on. The young Sir John prepared to go with him but Wallace stopped him, saying he had already lost too many men through recklessness and like a burnt child was afraid of fire. He promised Sir John he would send for him whenever he deemed the time ripe and needed his services. Meantime he intended to look up some friends in Clydesdale and plan his next move there. Sir John agreed to this, saying that whenever Wallace sent for him he would come as quickly as he could with all the strength he could muster.

Wallace rode out from Dundaff with his four companions. They made their way to Bothwell Muir where they stayed the night with a certain Crawford with whom they were safe. Next day they rode on to Gilbank where they were made very welcome by another uncle of Wallace, the Sheriff of Ayr's brother, young Affleck, who had married the lovely widow of Sir Ranald when he was murdered by the English. They had several children, as can be seen in the records of Lesmahago where they held some land. At that time they had to pay tribute for their own land to Lord Percy of Northumberland, under the deal made by the Sheriff.

Word soon reached Percy of the terrible setbacks the English in the Perth area were having at Wallace's hands: Kincleven burnt and rased to the ground, its captain slain, the captain of Perth also slain, Lorn slain at Shortwood Shaws, Butler and so many of his men – a long tale of woe.

Percy inquired into the details and his courier by no means understated the valour of Wallace – it had to be an outstanding man to excuse so much havoc. He said he was sure Wallace had not crossed Stirling Bridge, it was so well guarded, and hoped he had been drowned swimming the Forth. 'That would be a great pity,' said the valiant Percy, 'for it would seem that this is the greatest warrior now living and if we could win him to the king's side he might conquer an empire. I grieve that our knights have been slain, that is indeed a great blow. We must see to it that they are replaced at once. If your Wallace is all you say he is, I don't believe he is dead as we will soon learn to our cost. He knows the Forth too well and would not risk his life where the odds were against him crossing successfully. He obviously has brains as well as brawn.' And Percy sent a messenger to appoint Sir John Stewart to the Sheriffdom of Perth and all the land around it. But no attempt was made to restore Kincleven.

Meantime Wallace sent Kerlie to Sir Ranald with news of his latest doings, and also to his cousin Adam, and to Boyd and Blair. They were delighted to hear he was still alive and fighting and arranged to supply him from then on with all the money he needed.

John Blair, Master of Arts, was a worthy scholar, daring and wise as well as learned. He had long studied and taught in Paris among the famous masters there: he and Wallace had gone to the same school as boys. It is this John Blair who wrote the Latin biography of Wallace to which we are indebted here for so much of our material and history of Wallace, aided by Thomas Gray the priest of Liberton. Both knew Wallace well and were associated with him in some of his campaigns. When Blair heard the good news of Wallace he at once set off to see him and was overjoyed to find him in good health and spirits. He brought silver and gold with him and Wallace treated him to the best hospitality he could muster.

Despite Percy's forebodings, the English believed Wallace to be either dead or so reft of men and support as to be of little danger: but all true Scots rejoiced in their champion's survival and gave him all they could when they could. The truce made by the Sheriff of Ayr was still in force, having about four months more to run. Wallace stayed at Gilbank over the Christmas/New Year period, only leaving occasionally to go in disguise to Lanark for some amusement and relief. Any English he met going or coming never lived to tell the tale and many bodies were found with their throats cut or stabbed to the heart.

Now at that time, Lanark was oppressed by an English sheriff, Heselrig, a cruel and ruthless despot whose atrocious deeds made him feared by all the people. He was much puzzled by the deaths of so many of his countrymen and set up patrols and watch parties. These patrols caused Wallace and his four companions to tread more warily, and they always submitted to them when they couldn't be avoided, so that no suspicion fell on them.

Wallace Falls in Love

It was during these ploys in Lanark that the most momentous thing in all Wallace's personal life happened: he met and fell in love with a beautiful girl of good family, Mirren Braidfuit. She was the eighteen-year-old daughter of Hugh Braidfuit of Leamington, and, as both her father and mother had recently died, she inherited all his property and fortune, and lived alone with the family servants in their house in Lanark. As she paid tribute to King Edward she came under his peace and protection, living as quietly and safely as she might in such troubled times. Her brother, who should have inherited, had been slain by Heselrig on some pretext or other, so she had reason to hate the Sheriff. She was a girl of patient endurance, sweet-natured and unpretentious as well as good-looking, well-spoken and good-mannered: altogether a girl of exceptional qualities, and well-liked by all who knew her. Wallace happened to see her one day when she was going to church with a companion and was captivated immediately. He quickly found out all about her. He knew the Braidfuits well by reputation, and managed to get himself introduced. He was so smitten that he was awkward and restless in her company, scarcely knowing what on earth bothered him. All he knew for sure was that now she was never out of his mind, as if she had suddenly entered his life and could never leave it, as if she were some part of himself he had never known before and was now a person always at his side, if not in the flesh, as a constant presence. The invincible warrior was conquered, and by a girl, and he was quite unprepared for it.

Wallace was greatly troubled by this experience for it seemed to him incompatible with his destiny, his vocation to free the Scots from English dominion. How could he belong to Scotland and to a woman at the same time? Was it not through his affair, albeit a much shallower matter than this, which he knew to be no mere affair, that he had lost his dear companions? So at times he felt he must either give up his love for Mirren or his dedication to Scotland's cause. He felt pulled in two opposite directions, yet he also knew that he could give up neither – both came to him as undeniable experiences, demands of life that could not be denied without denial of the spirit, that unforgiveable sin. So, torn with distress and perplexity of soul, he confided his dilemma in the faithful Kerlie, asking him for his true and fearless advice.

'My dear commander,' said Kerlie, 'I don't really see why you make such a dilemma of the matter. You love the girl, well then, marry her. You love Scotland, well then, fight for it. She is a girl well deserving you, of independent means, and you can be quite sure she will never betray you as the Perth girl did. There's no comparison.' 'Marry her?' said Wallace. 'That's just it. I feel I cannot marry, it wouldn't be right, till I have cleared Scotland of the accursed English. No, I simply must not see her again – at least never be alone with her in case I can't control myself and am swept away by love against my better judgment. But once the war is over... well then if she is still free... Heavens, to be at the mercy of love, is it not just silly? It robs one of reason and determination. How can love and war live in me at the same time? If I were living in normal times with no quarrels other than those which arise in the ordinary course of a man's life, this blessed gift of love would strengthen me, not undermine me. My life and my love would be part of each other. But in present circumstances where great and serious purposes tax me beyond my ordinary powers, demand of me an effort and concentration beyond my natural capacities, a great country overrun by its enemies and deserted by its proper leaders, what right have I to indulge myself in the demands of love? I cannot serve both Scotland and a wife. Besides, it wouldn't be fair to a girl like Mirren to involve her in any way in this ruthless war: and not only her, but her family.'

Thus Wallace went on tormenting himself, but the more he argued against his love of Mirren, the stronger it grew. He was trapped in his destiny. He tried to keep away from her and from Lanark itself, but he only made himself miserable and depressed. Kerlie watched him for a time, but one day he felt it had gone far enough. 'My dear commander,' he said, 'I can't see you grow more and more languid and sad. For goodness sake go and see her and stop making yourself ill.'

Wallace bowed to the inevitable and sent a messenger to Mirren asking to see her. Meanwhile, it happened that things had become more difficult for Mirren herself. Not only had she always to watch her step among the English soldiery, but Heselrig himself, her brother's murderer, had taken a notion to marry her to his son. She therefore asked Wallace to come to her in secret. One of her maidservants brought him by a route through her garden. She had a meal waiting for him. Once in her presence all doubt left him and he embraced her, pouring out his heart and his love for her.

Wallace found Mirren as much against the English as himself, and as much in love with him as he with her. She made it clear that she would not become his mistress or that of any man, but if he felt her unworthy to be his wife, nevertheless she would serve him and his cause in every honourable way she could, trusting in his own honour not to take advantage of her. He could imagine how she had had to guard her honour surrounded as she was by enemies, and unprotected. 'I trust you will not dishonour me nor your own family, much less your worthy self,' she said.

'My dear,' said Wallace, deeply moved, 'there is no woman in this world I would more gladly marry than your own good self. I am honoured you should even think of me as a husband. But I am dedicated to freeing our country from the accursed yoke of the English and feel that a man in my position ought not to marry till the war is over. And of course I will make no other demand of you that might compromise your honour.' On that note they went into dinner, deeply in love, but with an understanding which was deepened by their talk over the meal. Then Wallace took his farewell of her and slipped away, heavy in heart with the pain of his love, and still grieving over the loss of his men.

Rejoining his four companions, they made haste to Gilbank while it was still daylight, to spend the night there. Next day they rode without halting to the Corheid where he had a cousin Edward Little and a nephew Tom Halliday. Right glad they were to see their noble kinsman alive, for they had heard a rumour that he had been slain at Strathearn. For three whole days they feasted and made merry, then Wallace decided he would like to take stock of the English strength in the town of Lochmaben. With his new friends, Wallace now had sixteen mounted men at his service but he left them all in the Knock Wood except Tom Halliday, Edward Little and the good Kerlie, who set out with him for Lochmaben. Tom knew the place well and led them straight to an inn where they ordered dinner. While it was being prepared, feeling reasonably safe, they went to hear mass in a nearby chapel.

It happened that a certain Englishman called Clifford came to the inn that day. He was a nephew of the overlord and had four men with him. As soon as he caught sight of the Scots party's horses in the courtyard he demanded to know who owned such well-harnessed, fine animals, and when he heard the owners were Scots, he was indignant. 'How the devil can Scots be so well-horsed? It seems they will never learn their proper place. It is time their arrogance was somewhat curtailed.' So saying, despite the pleas of the goodwife of the inn, he dismounted, drew his razor-edged dagger and sliced off the tails of the snorting, bellowing horses, amid the cries and protests of the goodwife. Hearing the noise, Wallace and his men came running back. Wallace took stock of the situation and marched up to Clifford who was tying up his own horse. 'I see you have a taste for jokes, my friend, as well as acting the horse-marshall. I don't recall asking this service of you, but as you have rendered it anyway I am minded to see you suitably rewarded for your trouble. You have the makings of quite a barber so I would like to show you how we Scots do the shaving and cutting business.' So saying he whipped out his sword and split Clifford's head open with one clean stroke, turned to meet another Englishman running up and struck the head from his shoulders. Meanwhile, his men had slain the others and they decided it was no time to wait for dinner. Binding up their horses' stumps they paid the goodwife and rode out of the town.

There was a great hullabaloo among the English when they found their lord's nephew had been slain, and a troop of veteran soldiers set out from the castle after Wallace, who did not let up till he had reached the Knock Wood. The horses were weakened by pain and loss of blood and the Scots dismounted and led them to a hillock where they could survey the land. About a mile away they could see the English troop, well over a hundred of them, speeding toward the wood. They mounted at once and headed north and east, meeting up with the rest of their men on the way through the wood. A small vanguard of mounted archers drew close enough to wound two of them with arrows. Seeing they were few, Wallace drew his men into a dell and waited for them, dashing out with drawn swords. Fifteen were slain almost at once, the others escaping back to the main body. Wallace was for chasing them but Halliday wisely pointed out the folly of such a move. Wallace curbed his anger and they retreated into the wood. It was clear to Wallace that a stand would have to be made before the English caught up and he chose to make it on a wooded hillock where at least they would have the advantage of fighting downhill, and the trees afforded some cover.

The first Englishman in the attack was a valiant warrior called Hugh of Moreland, said to be the best warrior in the North of England and the slayer of many an unlucky Scot. He was mounted on a noble charger and girt in armour of the finest steel. He picked out Wallace at once and rode full tilt at him. Wallace, seeing a formidable foe, kept close to a big oak tree he could easily dodge around, and waited. Moreland slackened pace because of the tree and rode in more slowly, making a ferocious slash at Wallace. The Scot easily side-stepped it and as the horse passed him the great five-foot sword whunnered through the air and hit Moreland on the shoulder, shearing through steel and bone. Wallace quickly took what he could of the fallen man's gear and his horse, leaving his own much weakened steed. Thus freshly mounted and armed, he rode about among the English dealing death with almost every blow. It was a fierce battle and it went to and fro at first but the English lost so many men and were so amazed at the berserk feats of slaughter wrought by Wallace himself that soon they fell back and finally took to their heels. Some thought such a man could retake Scotland almost single-handed, and if he could go on like that, he would. So they told their lord Graystock when they got back to the main troop post-haste.

Graystock had newly arrived in Scotland and still had his English arrogance untamed by experience of Wallace's whip. He did not imagine a Scot would dare oppose him, and was affronted by his stalwarts fleeing from a few Scots, even more so when he heard they had lost Moreland and many others. He decided to teach these insolent Scots a lesson they'd never forget, and set off after Wallace with some three hundred men.

Meanwhile the Scots, whose casualties were only five wounded, changed their tired horses for fresh ones taken on the field and sped on, Wallace and Halliday bringing up the rear. As they wanted to save the horses they did not overstretch them and the English vanguard began to overtake. Wallace was soon aware of them and took stock of their numbers, roughly, and of the position generally. Obviously the English would try to attack with their full strength and that must not be – they must be broken up somehow into smaller groups. But the English, apart from the Lord Graystock, were very careful to keep together as much as they could, knowing Wallace. Wallace and Halliday deliberately fell back from their own main body, letting the English van come near enough to see them quite clearly. Those who knew him were able to identify Wallace, who flaunted himself on Moreland's horse, and advised Graystock not to pursue this dangerous Scot any further. Graystock was enraged. 'What! flee from a handful of Scots!' he said. 'What a pack of cowards you are.' So saying he pressed on before his reluctant men, intent on forcing Wallace to a trial of strength. Wallace of course intended to avoid any such confrontation, but his horse began to tire and it became clear he couldn't make it to Queensberry. On the very outskirts of the town, as it happened, Sir John the Graham appeared with thirty stalwart warriors. He had spent the night at the Corheid and, not having heard from Wallace in all this time, was impatient for news of him. There he met in with one Kirkpatrick, a fierce warrior from Easdale Wood. He too was seeking news of Wallace and had twenty sturdy men with him – he was Lord of Torthorwold and related to Wallace on the Crawford side. They hadn't ridden far together when they heard the sound of battle and spurred forward to see Wallace beset by the English. Graham at once launched an attack with Kirkpatrick and all fifty men. Each one of them killed his man in that first onset before the English had time to realize what had hit them. Wallace was easily identified not only by his great stature but because, dismounted now, he fought with his mighty two-handed sword whirling a circle of death around him. The ferocity of the Scots was too much for the English soldiers and they fled, the arrogant Graystock leading the way on a powerful steed. The Scots pursued them determined on vengeance. Wallace shouted to Graham that it was folly to kill ordinary soldiers while the leaders escaped, and knowing that the best men would be around Graystock they concentrated on riding them down. Graham was better mounted than Wallace who encouraged him to outdistance the English, turn them, break them up, and scatter their formation. Graham and Kirkpatrick and their fastest men soon overtook the English and charged into them sideways, aiming at Graystock in the centre. After some fierce fighting

Graham himself got through to Graystock and at once attacked him with all his might. After some exchange of blows Graham caught Graystock on the neck with his heavy blade and sliced through armour into the bone. Graystock was dead before he hit the ground. Wallace and the others soon arrived and hurled themselves into the fight, Kirkpatrick and Halliday acquitting themselves particularly well that day of great deeds. The English were completely routed and sought cover in the forest.

When the Scots reassembled, Wallace and the Graham warmly renewed their mutual affection and comradeship. Wallace, who in the heat of the battle had shouted a rather angry order to Graham, now apologised and praised the other's valour. Graham for his part made light of the incident saying Wallace was quite right and that from now on he was to regard Graham as a son in military matters, lacking the wisdom and experience of his leader and father-in-arms. Wallace also thanked and praised Kirkpatrick, his cousin. It was indeed a happy chance that these two and their forces arrived on the scene when they did.

That night Wallace and his comrades, fired with new hope and zeal, discussed what their next move should be. Wallace, still mindful of the men he had lost in the past and chary of risking lives any more than he could help, tentatively suggested that they should try to take Lochmaben Castle. But he made it clear it was only a suggestion, and if others thought it too risky he would accept their opinion. He felt that the castle would now be practically undefended, and might be easily taken. Then, if they could go on to take Caerlaverock, still in the hands of Lord Maxwell, it would greatly strengthen their position in that area and discomfit the English. The Graham gave his hearty approval and the others added their agreement. Without any waste of time they rode off for Lochmaben Castle, halting about half a mile from it to prepare their plans. It was a pitch-dark night and they decided on immediate action. No sound was heard from the Castle and Wallace got Tom Halliday to ride ahead and take stock. Tom took a man called Watson with him who was well-enough known in Lochmaben to be useful. They both rode openly up to the gate and Watson called the porter, who knew his voice. The porter unsuspectingly opened the gate and Tom Halliday at once seized him by the throat and stabbed him to death. Watson took the keys off him and they threw the body into a hole near the gate. By this time Wallace and the others came up and they all ran silently into the castle. There seemed to be nobody there except for some women and a couple of servants, and the scullions they found and killed in the kitchen. Seeing this, the lady of the castle begged for mercy. 'Have no fear, madam,' said Wallace, 'I do not make war on women and children. Come, we are hungry, bring us some food. What say you, Halliday?' Various kinds of food and drink were soon brought and the hungry warriors ate like starving wolves. Sentries had been posted by the gate, and as men of the castle who had escaped the slaughter arrived in ones and twos they were quietly let in by Watson and slain. No man of English birth was allowed to live.

Next day Wallace and his men made a thorough survey of the castle, which was in very good shape. They stayed another night there, then having appointed one of Halliday's relatives captain of the castle, and left him an ample garrison, they set the women and children on the road to England, and they themselves headed for the Corheid. They spent the night there, then Wallace and the Graham set off for Crawford Muir, but not before making a hearty meal. Halliday, Kirkpatrick and others made their way back to their own homes without fear of molestation, or to hiding-places in hospitable woods. The two leaders took forty men with them and pressed on over the Crawford Muir till they came to the Clyde water about nightfall. There they planned their next moves in a quiet little glen and discussed the possibility of taking Crawford Castle. Graham thought it might be done if they could surprise it when the garrison were all out except for a few men. The Captain of Crawford Castle at the time was a Cumbrian squire, Martindale. Wallace decided that he should go ahead with one man to find an inn near the Castle where they could wait for an opportunity, while Graham and the others came on behind. As they neared an inn that might serve, they met and questioned a women who told them to keep well clear of it as it was occupied by the English, who were on the look-out for Wallace, having heard of his capture of Lochmaben. The woman was a patriotic Scot, though she did not know Wallace, and on quizzing her further they learned that the Castle was practically unguarded, the garrison being at the said inn – about twenty of them. Wallace signalled to Graham to come up and hastily conferred with him. 'Little and I can deal with the drunken garrison at the inn,' he said. 'You make for the castle now and we'll join you.' Then with Little guarding his back, he went into the inn. The garrison captain started up with an oath against the Scots, but he never spoke again – Wallace's sword went right through him. The other Englishmen were quickly slain, none escaping.

Wallace and Little then hastened after Graham to the castle and when they arrived they found Graham had set the gate on fire. Soon the Scots were swarming into the castle. They met only women, weeping and wailing in fear of their lives, and the children and a few servants. All were spared but expelled from the castle. There was very little food in the place, but they stayed the night there, bringing all they needed from the inn. Next day they took what gear and loot they could find, then set the castle on fire, destroying everything they could before riding off to Dundaff where they rejoiced at the good luck Providence had given them.

Chapter 6

Wallace Marries Mirren

After the dreary winter, when February had passed into March and March into April, Wallace left Dundaff and went to Gilbank. With the return of Spring and nature stirring with life and love, he felt his driving passion for Mirren Braidfuit unendurable. Despite the danger from the English presence there, he resolved to seek her out in Lanark. Whether time and suffering had resolved his conflict between Scotland and Mirren I know not, nor whether time had mellowed Mirren's conventional chastity I know not, but when they met they simply threw themselves into each other's arms, driven by a force of nature that bows to no superior. In the tempestuous passion of their bed of love all other lesser concerns were forgotten, and in the fusion of their souls through their bodies they were indissolubly married for all time before Church and State added their blessing. The old conflict returned at times, but during that honeymoon period Wallace simply pushed war into the background. He curbed his warlike spirit for over a year during which he and Mirren were blissfully happy as only true lovers can be, and before the year was up Mirren had borne him a daughter. This child grew up to be a fine woman who married a certain Squire called Shaw, and bore him fine sons. But the hand of destiny was on William Wallace and the old calling to war against the English oppressor began to clamour ever more loudly with every new atrocity he saw or heard of. He had no choice but to take up the sword again and follow his destiny.

Wallace and his wife had been lying low in the country all this time. Now he decided it was time to take a look at Lanark again, so he and the Graham, feeling that the English would be lulled by his long inactivity into a sense of security, went with a score or so companions, and slipped into the town in small numbers. They went to mass at a church there, fairly certain they would not be recognized, but the spies of Heselrig and his henchman Robert Thorn did in fact recognize Wallace and warned their master. Deciding to provoke Wallace, Heselrig sent some of his men to pick a quarrel with him. Led by a man of great strength, the English party began to mock the Scots who soon found themselves surrounded and far outnumbered. Wallace was trying to avoid open battle, not knowing the truth of things, but when he saw Heselrig himself approaching he knew there was no alternative. The Scots drew their weapons and fought like tigers, and Wallace picked on one particular ruffian who had been insulting the name of his wife, accusing her of lechery. He struck the sword hand off the lout to such effect that he was nearly blinded by the blood spouting from the stump. Graham finished the man off while Wallace wiped the blood out of his eyes. Wallace's great sword whunnered round his head dealing certain death to all who came within its sweep. But the Scots were hopelessly outnumbered and had to fight in retreat. They were near to Mirren's house and Wallace knew that they could escape through it and over a back wall and off to nearby woods. Wallace and Graham held the English at bay while all their men one by one escaped through the house, then they too followed, Mirren barring the door against the English and dragging furniture against it to hold them back. It is said that no less than fifty Englishmen were killed in that skirmish.

Heselrig Murders Mirren

The English hammered and battered at the door and after a time managed to break it down, forcing their way in. Heselrig ordered some men to follow the Scots and others to search the house. Mirren was found in an upper chamber behind a barred door and brought before Heselrig, who knew her well, and knew her to be the wife of William Wallace. When she was dragged in front of him he simply signalled to one of his men who stabbed her to death. Thus the light and lamp of love she had lit for William Wallace was put out forever. What words can express such terrible grief? One of the women servants of the household, returning to find the house empty and ravaged and her mistress dead, found out where he was hiding and brought him the dreadful news. Wallace's grief can be imagined. For three days he lay in his tent neither eating, sleeping, nor speaking to anyone, alone with the terrible anguish of his amputated soul. His men round him, led by Graham, shared his mourning, till on the third day, haggard and hollow-eyed, he emerged. Strong men wept. He looked at the ground dully then said gruffly, 'Enough, we cannae bring her back to life. Let mourning be and let our revenge be her obsequies.' But he himself could not keep back the tears, and through broken sobs he swore, 'Never shall I rest until this outrage is avenged on the blackhearted monster who has done it. I vow to almighty God that never will I spare any Englishman capable of arms who comes within reach of my sword. For her life ten thousand will die!'

Hearing of Wallace's cruel bereavement, Auchinleck left his home in Gilbank and came to Cartland Wood with ten men. He arrived in the darkness of night and he and Wallace laid plans to seek out the criminal Heselrig immediately.

Wallace is Revenged on Heselrig and the English

The English did not expect so swift an attack nor so late. The Scots divided into two parties. One under the Graham sought out Sir Robert Thorn, the other under Wallace made straight for Heselrig's own house. They found it undefended outside and Heselrig himself was asleep: all was in darkness. Knowing his quarry so near, Wallace was filled with the rage and strength of ten. He ran at the big door and with one mighty kick burst it open and ran inside. Heselrig, leaping from bed at the crash, shouted, 'Who the devil's that?' 'A man you have been wanting to see all day and who is here to grant your wish, woman-killer – William Wallace.' Heselrig tried to escape in the darkness but Wallace was on him like a hound on a hare, and his terrible stroke split his head right down to the collar-bone. Then Wallace hurled the corpse over the stair and Auchinleck who was below, stuck his dagger three times in that black heart. Heselrig's son was next to fall to Wallace's avenging sword, and he too was thrown over the stair. Then the Scots dashed out into the street and began the slaughter of every Englishman they could find. Meantime, the Graham had set Thorn's house on fire and Thorn himself died in that blazing pyre, burned to ashes. It was said that over two hundred Englishmen were slain that night of wrath, and the women and priests were driven out of Lanark on pain of death if they ever returned.

When the Scots near and far heard of this purging of Lanark they flocked to Wallace and reoccupied Lanark, their own heritage. The Scots now looked to Wallace as their natural leader in the great struggle to free Scotland from the tyranny of the English. They had little hope of support from their own nobles, too many of whom were compromised with the English. Aylmer de Valence, that sly tyrant, was a willing stooge of Edward. He lived in

Bothwell at that time. Murray, the lord of the district, was an absentee landlord as everybody knows. He shunned the mainland and kept himself hidden away in Arran, like so many who were afraid to show their faces on the mainland. Aylmer de Valence now sent the news to his master Edward, warning him against the rising power of the Scottish hero and his successes against the English invaders. Edward was enraged at the news and sent his agents throughout England to raise an army against Wallace and his Scots in their own land.

It is said that Edward's queen Eleanor pleaded with her husband not to go on this expedition against the Scots as he would be committing a crime against a great Christian people whose crown was theirs of right. If so, her husband ignored her pleas and prepared for the invasion of his smaller neighbour. No Christian conscience deterred the unscrupulous tyrant in his wicked designs against the Scots.

One of the renegade Scots at that time serving in Edward's entourage, moved to shame by the news of Wallace's heroic action, slipped away one night and rode for Scotland to warn the great commoner of Edward's planned invasion. There seems to be confusion about his name but he came from Riccartoun in Kyle and the English called him Grimsby. He sought out Wallace as soon as he arrived in Scotland and was to prove a valuable man in times to come. He was familiar with various districts of England, from Hull to Bristol, Dover to St Bees Head, Carlisle to Sandwich and beyond. He was a man of great stature, middle-aged, and gave Wallace much valuable information about England and the English. Wallace was taken with his mental and physical powers and made him the bearer of the Arms of Scotland, a position of great trust. The man dropped the name Grimsby and adopted that of Jopp, by which the Scots knew him.

Wallace rode again into Clydesdale and there gathered as large an army as he could. He was now such a portent and power in the land that men flocked to him, and Wallace, like a king, offered to accept into his peace all who came to him, forgiving any previous fraternising with the enemy they may have been guilty of. Although the truce Sir Ranald, his uncle, had made with Percy had not yet expired, that knight sent his nephew his whole armed force, though he himself was unable to join him, and other kinsmen of Wallace sided openly with their great relative. Adam Wallace came from Riccartoun, as did Robert Boyd, with many true and stalwart men. A thousand horse came from Kyle and Cunningham. Sir John the Graham of course brought all his cavalry, Sir John of Tinto brought every man he could round up, as did Wallace's uncle the good Auchinleck. In all he had over three thousand fully armed men and many more lightly armed infantry all gathering in Lanark.

The Battle of Biggar

Edward of England soon arrived at Biggar with an army of some sixty thousand armed men, a most awesome sight. They set tents and pavilions everywhere and the air rang with the clamour of their trumpets. They also had an abundance of meat and drink which they brought with them in carts and wagons. The awesome king sent two heralds to seek out Wallace and order him to come at once and surrender unconditionally to him. 'Tell him,' he said, 'that because he is by birth a gentleman he may trust himself in safety to my grace. I will myself be responsible for his life; and if he will come into my service I shall see that he is properly rewarded.' By this double-talk Edward meant that if Wallace trusted the seemingly gracious old villain he would be put to death as a traitor.

There was a young nephew of King Edward, a Fitzburgh, who decided to go in disguise with the heralds in hope of seeing this notorious rebel William Wallace. Disguised in an assumed coat of arms he rode with them to Tinto Hill where, scouts had informed Edward, Wallace stayed with his men. They were brought into the presence of Wallace and stated their purpose, giving him the king's message, in writing. Wallace called together the three knights in his army and read the message to them. He then said to the heralds, 'How would you like my reply: by word of mouth or in writing?' They said they would prefer it in writing. Wallace sat down at a camp table and began to write: 'King of robbers, you who command me in my own country where you have no right to be with or without your army of brigands to come and surrender to what you call your grace, if I were fool enough to trust you I'd be hanged, drawn and quartered. I swear to God that if I ever get my hands on you it is you who will be hanged for your crimes against the Scots. YOU offer me reward! The only reward I look for is to see you and your villainous people driven out of Scotland. I defy you and your power. I am coming against you tomorrow before nine o'clock to take you if I can for your crimes against this kingdom.' He then gave the letter to the heralds and gave them the customary tip. It happened that Jopp came along just as they were going and he knew the king's nephew despite his disguise. He at once warned Wallace who ordered all three to be seized. 'My vengeance first will fall on you,' he said to the young squire, 'who dare to assume arms.' And he had the young man beheaded at once. And because the heralds had also deceived him he had the tongue of one cut out and the eyes of the other. He then sent them back to Edward bearing the head of his nephew. That's how little William Wallace feared the powerful and ruthless King Edward: he talked back to him in his own language.

When the heralds reached Edward the king went nearly out of his mind with fury, rampaging and cursing and swearing in rage that anybody should dare to treat HIM like that. When his fit had subsided he swore the most terrible revenge on Wallace and the Scots before ever he saw England again.

Wallace meantime decided to check up on the English forces himself and he rode in disguise towards Biggar. On the way he met a tradesman selling pots and such, and asked him where he was going. The man replied he was on his way to sell his wares to anybody who would buy. Wallace said he'd buy the lot, horse and all and gave the man far more than he asked for them. Wallace also took the man's hooded cloak and so disguised himself as a seller of earthenware. It was already twilight as they came in among the English round Biggar, and as the poor pot-seller went to and fro among them he noted everything worth noticing, particularly the royal pavilion where Edward lived and those of the great barons round about. He came in for a lot of banter and horseplay from the English but managed to get away all right and back to his own camp. There he gathered his chiefs, Graham and Tinto among them, and told them of his exploits and all that he had noticed. The Graham reproached Wallace for his foolhardiness: it was not for the leader so to risk his own life on what a more expendable man might have done as well. But Wallace just said they would all have to take far greater risks than that, and that it was time now to get some sleep.

They slept till dawn, then all the Scots armed themselves and got into battle array. They then marched down from Tinto Hill, Wallace himself leading the way, flanked by Boyd and Auchinleck. Once in the plain, Wallace divided his force into groups under various leaders, Graham, Adam and young Somerville among them. He had about three thousand men in all, and one thousand he put under each of three captains, and of these the least well armed thousand he put in the rear, telling them to watch for a time and place where they might effectively come in. He warned them all against being distracted from their main purpose of destroying the English into looting the dead of gear and valuables. 'The more you kill,' he told them, 'the more there will be for you afterwards and the easier it will be for you to collect it. It won't run away, have no fear, and there will be more than enough for you all. Put honour, worthiness, the rights of your forebears first, and by God's grace we may yet win back our inheritance from these villainous people.'

As they moved against the mighty English army they saw a company of about three hundred men in flashing armour marching directly towards them. Wallace soon perceived that they were not English but recognisably Scots. They were in fact from Annandale and they were ably led by Tom Halliday, and his two sons. Wallace and his men were much heartened by the sight of such stalwarts coming to their side. Jordan and Kirkpatrick also joined them in a wing of Wallace's own company.

The English watch had no sleep that night but kept up a constant vigil while the army rested. When the dawn broke they rejoined the main body. Wallace knew well where the king's pavilion was, and drew his own force as near to it as he could, his best cavalry in the van. Giving the English no time to form up, no parley of scouts or heralds, the Scots charged at once, aiming straight for Edward's pavilion. The cavalry wrought terrible havoc among the enemy in that first thundering charge, the slaughter was horrific and the English broke before they had time to properly form up. The other companies of Scots were attacking at the same time from different angles and the English lords had difficulty trying to get some order into the resulting confusion among their men.

The most experienced of them saw at once the danger to the king and rallied around his menaced pavilion to defend it. The Earl of Kent, who was some distance away, made for the king with his five thousand well armed men. The battle became fierce and bloody, both sides hard pressed, but the English tents were brought to the ground, often smothering men inside. Seeing the confusion, the thousand light-armed Scots footmen came in among the English footmen, adding to their already sorry plight. They stole what arms they needed from the fallen enemy and made good use of them to increase the number of dead.

The ferocity of the Scots attack on the King's pavilion broke through the English ranks and the tent was brought to the ground, exposing Edward himself to great danger. But his knights, led by the stalwart Earl of Kent, formed an impenetrable wall round the King who was now forced to mount and prepare to flee. Kent wielded a mighty battle-axe almost as effectively as Wallace wielded his double-handed sword, and Wallace realised that Kent had to be brought down. He hammered his way through to that mighty warrior and after an exchange of blows Wallace's sword caught Kent on the neck and all but took the head from his shoulders. The King was reluctant to flee, but his knights forced him to do so, hauling his horse's reigns against his will. Edward and his bodyguard got away but it is said they left four thousand of their men slain on the battlefield.

As the sun mounted the sky that brilliant, clear day, Wallace stopped to take stock of the situation. The English had been confused by the suddenness and ferocity of the Scots attack and by its unorthodox tactic of striking at the heart of the English army. Now the still huge army was being organised around the King and Wallace deemed it unwise to try his luck any further. He therefore called his men together and turned back to Biggar where they plundered not only the dead of their gear but took all the provisions, gear, jewellery, money and the like which had been abandoned in the flight. Every Scot that day became something of a wealthy man and right heartily they feasted on Edward's rich provender. Then Wallace set up a body of sentinels to keep watch over the army.

There were two English cooks feigning dead among the slain, and when they saw their chance they got up and slunk away in the night, hoping to rejoin what was left of the English army.

After a few hours sleep Wallace, ever wary of English trickery, addressed his men. 'The English will no doubt come after us before long and if would be folly to meet them in pitched open battle, especially on this flat ground. So we must ride on till we find a much stronger position.' Then, sending most of the loot to Ropis Bog, he and his army set off for Daw's Wood and stayed there most of the day.

Meanwhile Edward retreated to Coulter Hope, and when he was satisfied that the Scots were not pursuing him, camped in Johnny's Green. There, once the stragglers were all in, he took stock and went mad with rage, in his usual maniacal way, to find his losses so great. In particular he had lost two uncles, his second son, and his brother Hugh – an irreparable loss which he lamented for the rest of his life. The two cooks who had feigned dead now arrived at the camp and told Edward the Scots were lying dead drunk on the king's own wine, and could easily be slaughtered in their drunken sleep. Edward was not impressed. He told them Wallace was too good a captain to be caught out like that and the loss of their provisions made it imperative the English must press on home. But the Duke of Longcastle was all for having a go at the Scots, for if they could be taken so easily they'd get all the provisions back and not need to go home at all. But the king was adamant that he would not go back after the

Scots. Longcastle then asked him for a detachment of some thousands of troops saying he would go back and deal with the Scots while the king stayed here. Edward agreed to this and they set off for Biggar where they were met by Sir Ralph Gray and the traitor Sir Aylmer de Valence. Nothing but dead bodies lay on the field but Sir Aylmer's spies said they had seen the Scots make for Daw's Wood. The English advanced in that direction but when Wallace's sentinels spied them coming, Wallace decided to move his army to Ropis Bog, where a stand on foot could be made. The Scots horses were tethered in a wood nearby.

When the English came up and saw the Scots formed up in the bog they thought they'd have a walk-over. They charged on horseback but soon found themselves bogged down in the deep swamp where, in their helplessness, they were fallen upon by the Scots and massacred, the lightclad Scots footmen being unhampered by the armoury of the cavalry knights. Wallace tried personally to slay Aylmer de Valence but was prevented by Lord Westmoreland. In the ensuing duel Wallace slew Westmoreland, cleaving right through his helmet into his skull. But meantime, de Valence had made his escape. When the Duke got back to Edward with news of the disaster, Edward was madder than ever, and vowed terrible vengeance on William Wallace. He took the rest of his army over the Solway and out of Scotland for the time being. The Scots plundered the dead, rested the night nearby and then pressed on to Braidwood where they held a council of war for three whole days.

Wallace is Made Guardian of Scotland

The council decided to hold a full-scale meeting at Forest Kirk, and there Wallace was appointed Guardian of Scotland and entrusted with the task of bringing the evils of the English occupation to an end. Wallace received all those willing to come into his peace, including Sir William Douglas, who came over from Edward, disgusted with his experience of English bondage. Sir William had paid tribute money to the English but had never taken arms against the Scots, so Wallace had no difficulty in welcoming so distinguished and powerful a lord into the cause. All loyal Scots who came over to the cause and accepted Wallace as Guardian were well-treated and given a share of what spoil the Scots had won from the invaders. But he set a stern face against all those who rebelled against him and the cause, dealing severely with all who fell into his power, no matter what their rank. In this way he became the effective and successful government of Scotland, and good government it was – fair, wise, strong, manly, liberal and good-hearted. The country began to recover its lost prosperity. Wallace set up sheriffs and captains throughout much of the country. A castle at Wigton held out against him for a while, but when the captain heard that Wallace was marching against him he escaped by sea to England and Wallace put Adam Gordon into the castle in his place. One or two other castles gave some trouble, one on the Cree and Turnberry for instance, but they were soon brought under and the Scots were able to rest at Black Crag in Cumnock for three months. The English decided it might be best to play for time by seeking a truce and to this end they sent for the traitor Aylmer de Valence who still held out in Bothwell. Lord Percy still dominated Ayr and supported Bishop Beck in Glasgow.

The Truce of Rutherglen

The Earl of Stamford, the English Chancellor, charged Sir Aylmer de Valence with the task of making a truce with Wallace. Wallace was induced to promise de Valence a safe conduct for the purpose of truce talks and they met in Ru'glen Kirk on an agreed day. Stamford himself accompanied de Valence, and Wallace took with him a picked troop of fifty men, all clad in forest green, with bows and arrows as well as their long swords. Wallace first heard mass in the Kirk with his men. They then formed up before the altar to await the English party. Wallace bristled with anger at sight of Aylmer de Valence but curbed his anger in terms of his promise. But the set mask of his stern face chilled the English with fear. Stamford began to doubt his own wisdom in facing so heroic a man, but de Valence told him he need have no fear to open negotiations as Wallace would not break his word for the whole of England let alone one man. The chancellor was reassured and offered the hero his hand. Wallace stood stonily refusing to acknowledge the gesture. At this de Valence said, 'Wallace, this is the Earl of Stamford, Chancellor of England. It is but courtesy to take his hand.' Wallace thought for a minute and replied, 'Your master can have at any time such greeting as I habitually give the English who come within reach of my sword, that I swear to God, and I wish right now I were not disarmed by my bond, which nevertheless I shall not break. As for you, you damned traitor, I wish I had you without this safe conduct that I might be avenged on you for the vile wrongs you have done your country – I'd give a king's ransom for that pleasure. But I will honour my bond. Get on with it, Chancellor, with no more delay.'

Stamford then told him that his main purpose was to seek peace and that he had been sent by King Edward with his great seal and backed by Parliament. Whatever the Chancellor bound himself to with Wallace would be binding also on the great lords of England and the king himself.

Wallace replied that his conditions would be that the English give up all claim to Scotland and withdraw all

English troops still holding out. Stamford said he had no authority for such an agreement but that he had gold with him to indemnify the Scots – in other words, to bribe them. Wallace told him he was wasting his time, he sought neither gold nor favours from the English: he would take all he wanted of English gear and gold by force of arms. At this the chancellor fell silent. He was up against a man who knew no compromise and could not be bargained with. Wallace then went on to say that there was no point wasting more time, but, for the sake of giving the poor Scots peasantry a rest from war and time to try to recover from its ravages he would agree to a truce for one year only. So although peace had not been achieved and could not be achieved without the English foregoing all claim to Scotland, at least a truce in the continuing war was agreed. Stamford and Wallace sealed this bond and went their ways. Each castle and town was to remain as it now was for one year. Stamford returned south and Wallace rode over to his uncle Sir Ranald to tell him the news, then went on to his own place in Cumnock. But he had little faith that the English would keep their word.

Chapter 7

The truce of Ru'glen was made in February, but by April
the English were breaking it in various ways. King
Edward left his palace in Cumberland and came to
Carlisle where he held a council against the Scots. The
only Scot at the council was the traitor Aylmer de
Valence, who was asked how to deal with all the Scots
lords who refused to submit themselves and their
hereditary lands to Edward. Sir Aylmer said that this
would be difficult now because Wallace had acquired such
power and authority that a new self-confidence had
emerged among the Scots. But he had a plan which might
undermine them and work the king's will. Thus the
traitor plotted against his own people with their
implacable enemy. The idea was to get as many of the
Scots lords as possible to come into four big barns in Ayr
which Edward had built for his own use and slay them
there without warning. Lord Percy protested at this
breach of good faith, saying that the Scots lords had
faithfully kept their part of the bargain, and he refused to
take part in the plot. So Edward made Arnulf, Earl of
Southampton, a reigning judge, with power to hang the
Scots for alleged treason. King Edward retired to the
south again but Arnulf, in the manner of the time, called
a travelling court for the eighteenth of June at Ayr. In
terms of the truce many Scots lords could be called to this
court and so they were, though many were outraged by
the English arrogance, considering the truce. Lord Percy
rode on to Glasgow, which alerted some Scots to some

anti-Scots ploy afoot which Percy could not stomach. Wallace and his uncle met the day before the court at Monkton Kirk.

Wallace Has a Vision

Wallace went into Monkton Kirk to worship, but having said the Lord's Prayer, the Hail Mary and the Creed, he suddenly fell into a deep sleep. His companion Kneland saw this and kept watch over him. Now in this sleep Wallace had a dream in which an old man came up to him and grasped his hand, saying he had a message for him. He gave Wallace a sword of burnished steel and told him to make good use of it. He then took Wallace up a high mountain from where he could see the whole world stretched out before him. The old man left him there, but Wallace wished he had remained, as he wanted to ask him questions. He could see Scotland in particular, the whole realm in a state of war and turmoil, and it seemed to be on fire from Ross to the Solway. As he brooded on the sight he saw a great luminous ball coming down from the sky towards him, coming nearer and nearer till it filled his whole vision and landed right beside him. Then he saw the light was in fact a lady dazzlingly bright. She handed him a wand of red and green, and taking a sapphire of dazzling blue she made the sign of the saltire cross upon his face. 'My love,' she said, 'I have chosen you to be my champion, and God will grant you the power to help the poor and oppressed people of Scotland. Go to them, your dearest kindred in their pain, redeem them and your dear land. Bitter will be your reward on earth for this great deed, but in heaven you will have eternal bliss and the lasting gratitude of your people. I must go now, but do not forget me, my love, my true knight, fight well in my cause.' Then she gave him a book and was gone in a ball of light up into the sky again.

Wallace opened the book and saw that it was written in three parts. The first part was in big brass letters, the second was in gold, and the third in shining silver. In his eagerness to read the writing, Wallace came out of the trance. Seeing the priest nearby he told him of his vision and asked what it might mean. 'My son,' said the priest, 'who am I to unravel such mysteries of God? I might lead you astray by misinterpreting. Yet I would risk saying that it seems to me that the old man who gave you the sword was St Andrew, patron saint of Scotland, and he means you to fight for your country's cause. I am uncertain who the lady is. She might be Fortune – she might even be Our Lady Mary, mother of Our Lord. That seems likeliest, though she might be Scotia, the mother of our people. If it was Our Lady, then she clearly is interceding with God for Scotland and has chosen you as her champion in Scotland's cause. The wand is the sceptre of government, red with blood shed in just war, green for nature and the land, the rightness of your cause. The blue sapphire is eternal grace with which you are blessed. The book is Scottish history, the brass of misfortune, the gold of honour and worth, the silver purity of life and assurance of heaven's bliss. More I cannot say, and may God have so guided my tongue that I speak the truth and not some calamitous error.'

Wallace thanked the good man and left the church, riding home to Crosby with his uncle. He was in a rapt state of wonder at his remarkable vision all that night.

Next day they were due at the district court and rode out till they came to Kingace. Here Wallace felt such strong misgivings about the whole business that he stopped and told his uncle about it. Would the English keep their bond? Where was the parchment on which the truce was sealed? His uncle assured him that it was safe in a trunk at Crosby, but told him if he was in any doubt about it he ought to ride back and reassure himself.

Wallace said he would be happier if they had the thing with them, in case of English treachery, and as no other person knew of its whereabouts he rode back. In this may be seen the providence of God.

English Treachery at Ayr

The same grace and providence of God did not attend Sir Ranald. All unsuspecting he rode up to the barns and through the gate assigned to him. At once a noose fell over his head, was drawn tight, and he was hanged from a baulk which had been set for the purpose. Sir Bryce the Blair was the next victim of the trap, then his uncle. Then came the gentle knight Sir Neil Montgomery. One after the other our Scots knights were hanged by the English in this devilish plot: many Crawfords died, Kennedys of Carrick, Campbells, Barclays, Boyds, Stewarts. Each and all were strung up on the baulk, then the dead bodies slung in a heap in the corner. It was an unparalleled atrocity even for the accursed English. When the news broke it dazed all Scotland with anger, incredulity, and horror. The flower of the nobility had been murdered by the vilest treachery in a time of truce. It called for a vengeance equally terrible, and as they recovered from the shock the Scots began to search for a plan of revenge. The nobles were even denied decent burial.

The worthy Robert Boyd took twenty of his best men to a certain inn loyal to Wallace and waited there. Stephen of Ireland learned from a woman in the street what had happened at the district court and she told him to tell Wallace to keep out of town meantime. He and his friends made for Laglane Wood. Wallace himself, uneasy about his friends, was on his way to the barns when the woman Stephen had met saw him and called out to him. When Wallace heard the story he was shocked and angered, especially for his own uncle and kinsmen. He then sent the woman to tell Boyd and his other men to meet him at Laglane Wood, and turned his own horse in that direction.

As he was riding along deep in mourning and anger he was seen by a party of fifteen Englishmen, all mighty warriors, and followed. Deciding to arrest him, they rode up to him. Wallace at once drew his long sword and furiously rode to meet them. He had three companions with him and between them they soon slew all the English except one or two who fled as fast as they could ride when they saw the fate of the others. When the English heard the news from these fugitives they lamented that Wallace had escaped the trap laid for him and the nobles. One old English knight said that with Wallace still alive the whole plot had been in vain and would be dearly paid for. The English Justice who was responsible for the atrocity proposed to give the lands and titles of the slain Scots nobles to as many Englishmen. They settled in the town for the night, sleeping in the big barns which they had used to trap the Scots. It is said there were about four thousand English in Ayr that night, with an abundance of provisions. Sure of their safety for the time being they set no watch that night, but celebrated their success, as they deemed it, drinking and carousing till they fell into a drunken sleep.

The woman did as Wallace told her, contacting as many Scots as she could and telling them all to go to Laglane Wood. Then she went there herself with news of the state of the drunken English. Wallace then gathered together some three hundred men, appointed Boyd, Crawford, Adam of Riccarton and Auchinleck leaders with him, and they made a plan of revenge. The woman was sent back to the town with chalk to mark the door of every known Englishman. Then twenty men with ties followed her and bound tight every door she had marked.

They also secured the big barns, silently and stealthily. Then straw and other kindling materials were heaped around the doors and walls, and at a signal were set ablaze. Wallace and his men spread out round the fires to cut down any man who might manage to break through. The dry tinder caught at once and the flames were soon soaring. Soon the cries of the English mingled with the roaring of the flames and outside the barn where he knew the English Justice was trapped Wallace shouted above the uproar JUSTICE – I'LL GIVE YOU JUSTICE! Inside the English were suffering the fires of hell before as well as after death. The trapped Englishmen tore at doors that were bound fast on the outside, and the few who did manage to break out were at once cut down by the waiting Scots. The cries of men were more like the roaring of beasts as they died, maddened and wild with pain and fear. Those who were killed trying to escape were thrown back into the flames.

Thus Wallace was avenged for the atrocity of the barns of Ayr, and it is said that the foul stench of burning flesh was so bad that it turned the stomachs even of the strongest men.

The Friar's Blessing

That same night it happened that a party of Englishmen, about seventy in all, were out of town and on riding back saw the conflagration and the Scots ring of steel. So they slunk off to the nearby priory and sought refuge there with Prior Drumlay for the night. The Prior had no choice but to let them in and allot the various cells, nine or ten per cell. He waited till they were asleep in the middle of the night then got his fellow friars together, about eight in all. The English had been persuaded to leave their weapons in a heap in the hall, and each friar now armed himself according to his fancy. Then each opened a cell and fell upon the sleeping men inside with murderous fury, stabbing and slicing at them. Most of them were killed but some escaped naked into the night, unaware who had attacked them, and some of them were drowned trying to cross the river. This deed became famous as the Friar of Ayr's Blessing.

How Beck and Percy were Hunted out of Glasgow

Boyd and his men soon took the castle of Ayr which was all but deserted and put the few remaining English there to the sword. So when Wallace and his men gathered together again after the holocaust of the barns of Ayr, in which the English dead ran into thousands, he directed their attention to Glasgow where Bishop Beck and Lord Percy were fortifying it and laying in stores. After they had all eaten, they took the best of the horses left by the English so that all three hundred men were well-mounted and they rode off for Glasgow where they crossed the wooden bridge over the Clyde unchallenged. But word soon reached Percy who at once prepared his army. Bishop Beck, although a priest, commanded a thousand armed men. Wallace's spies informed him of the numbers the enemy had mustered and he divided his force into two companies. One of these under Auchinleck and Adam Wallace he sent to enter the town from the rear while he and Boyd rode boldly forward into the streets. The English were amazed at the small number of Scots who came against them, and crying, 'A Percy, a Percy,' they rode out to meet them. The clash of arms was like striking fire from flint. Percy and Beck fought bravely, and as the second company of Scots attacked the English from the rear, Wallace strove hard to get to Percy himself. After much effort he found himself face to face with the mighty

Percy and after some passes Wallace's powerful stroke caught Percy on the helmet shearing through steel and bone. The great lord was dead. This knocked the fight out of the English and they fled with Beck in their midst, making for the woods nearby, hoping to press on to Bothwell Castle. Wallace followed, harrying the rear and stragglers. But Beck and Aylmer de Valence got safely into Bothwell. The castle was proof against immediate attack, so Wallace turned and rode to Dundaff where he told Sir John the news of the murders at Ayr before taking a well-earned rest. He stayed there for about five days till he received disturbing news from the highlands where the English had stirred up Buchan, Atholl, Menteith and Lorne against the loyal Argyll.

Wallace Kills Old Rukby at Stirling

The good knight Campbell was still holding out against Edward and his men. But there was a man MacFadyan, a lackey of the English king, who was set against him. This MacFadyan had been given overlordship of Lorn and Argyll by Edward, the traitor John of Lorn having conceded his own heritage to Edward in return for lands in England. Duncan of Lorn however still held out until MacFadyan beat him and forced him to flee to refuge with the good Campbell. Thus MacFadyan attained power in Scotland, and a hellish tyrant he proved to be. He had about fifteen thousand men to work his evil will, many of them ruthless Irishmen who spared neither women nor children, laying waste the country wherever they went, like wild beasts, burning and killing. With this crew of hellions MacFadyan invaded the Campbell lands of Lochawe. The good knight made a valiant stand at Craig Bhuidhe in the pass of Brander, with only three hundred men, and held it against violent attacks. He destroyed the bridge over the Awe so that the enemy would have to cross by a ford where the passage was very restricted. There Campbell bravely awaited them. The river was deep and broad except at this narrow ford. MacFadyan fretted at the river edge but saw the risk to his men if they tried to cross: they could ride only three or four abreast and Campbell could cut them down as they emerged. So, as game was plentiful round about, he decided to camp where he was for a while.

In this time of need Duncan of Lorn left Campbell to hold out while he himself went in search of Wallace, hoping to get his help. They were old school friends from Wallace's Dundee days. Duncan and his companion, an old man called Gilmichael, soon learned where to find Wallace and sought him out at once. When Wallace heard the news he gathered about him the Earl Malcolm, Richard of Lundy, Sir John the Graham and other leaders and prepared to set off to relieve Campbell. Wallace wanted to settle accounts with the villain MacFadyan.

Now Stirling Castle at that time was held by Rukby, and he greatly oppressed the folk round about. Wallace received word that Rukby was in a certain valley with a company of men, and he decided to try to ambush him, dividing his men into several small companies. Earl Malcolm took some of these men and lay in ambush at a certain spot. Wallace took a hundred men and set himself as bait for the trap by riding through Stirling in full sight of the English, up to Stirling bridge. There Rukby saw them and seeing the Scots were so few in number, he rode after them with about seven score good men at full gallop. As they came on, Wallace slew the leader with a fine spear he had in hand, then drew his sword and laid on. The Graham also speared a leader and drew his sword. The English archers brought down horses among the Scots, including the Graham's. Wallace dismounted and fought on foot to such effect that the English began to retreat before the Scots and so were driven into the ambush laid by Earl Malcolm. Wallace, who always sought out the most powerful man of the enemy, now pressed hard on Rukby and managed to confront him in personal combat. After a few exchanges Wallace's sword gave Rukby his death-wound and he fell to the ground. His two sons made their escape among the rest, and only twenty men got back alive to the castle.

Stirling Castle Falls to Earl Malcolm

Wallace set Malcolm to besiege the castle with his men, with orders to take it and hold it, while he pressed on after MacFadyan eager for revenge. MacFadyan was a commoner but valued by Edward as a good stooge for his tyrannous rule. Wallace gathered some two thousand men for the campaign and crossed Stirling Bridge and pressed on towards Argyll. Duncan of Lorn was their reliable guide. Back at the castle, the two sons of Rukby soon realised that with so few men and provisions they could not even hold Stirling Castle for long and they sought terms with Earl Malcolm. Malcolm promised them all their lives and an unmolested passage into England if they surrendered to him without bloodshed. So it was on the third day after Wallace left, that the castle came again into Scottish hands and the Rukby brothers survived to fight again in Scotland against the Bruce in later years.

Duncan of Lorn sent his man Gilmichael to scout in advance, for he knew the country well. By the time the Scots had passed Strath Fillan the small folk on foot began to tire of the weary march, and so indeed did the horses. Wallace therefore decided to take his best-mounted men and press on ahead, leaving the others to follow at a more leisurely pace. He and Graham each took a hundred of the best men, and Richard of Lundy five hundred. Five hundred were left behind altogether, and the rest followed on at their own pace. Wallace's party soon disappeared over the mountain pass. In Glendochart they were met by Gilmichael and the Lord Campbell himself, at the head of three hundred men. Gilmichael was sent forward again and, seeing one of MacFadyan's scouts, chased him and slew him before he could tell any tales. MacFadyan and his men lay at Loch Dochart in a narrow glen with no escape but one entry. Wallace and his men, dismounting and stealing up quietly, managed effectively to block their only means of escape. The enemy were trapped between deep water and craggy cliffs, and taken by surprise as the Scots fell on them. The ensuing struggle was hard-fought and merciless. Many a tyrant fell to rise no more. Wallace had a great steel staff in hand and did lethal work with it all round him. Campbell, the Graham, Lundy, Adam Wallace and Robert Boyd also did heavy work that day among the enemies of Scotland. MacFadyan and his Irish fought like tigers and held out for two long hours and more, hard-pressed by the Scots. Gradually however, the Scots made inroads into the Irish, and a terrible amount of blood was shed that day, until at last they broke and sought to escape. Many were drowned in the loch, while others tried to climb the cliff and were killed. The Scots among the enemy fell on their knees and begged for mercy and to be taken into Wallace's grace. Angry as he was, Wallace spared them and admonished them for their treachery. MacFadyan himself with some fifteen men escaped to a cave they knew high under Craigmore, like a fox gone to ground. Duncan of Lorn asked Wallace for the privilege of digging him out and slaying him and all with him. Wallace granted this. Soon the head of the tyrant was brought back on the point of a spear, and Lord Campbell had it set up on Craigmore. All the Scots who came over to Wallace had their lands restored to them and were made to swear fealty to his cause.

The Council in Ardchattan

Wallace gave all the Lorn lands to the faithful Duncan, telling him to hold them for Scotland. He then proclaimed a council to meet in Ardchattan. Many true Scots assembled there at the call of their Guardian, coming in from all parts of the country. Among them was a certain worthy knight, Sir John Ramsay of Ochterhouse, who was also a sheriff. He had always avoided submission to or compromise with Edward and had with great difficulty maintained his independence. He had about sixty men with him. He had held out in Strathearn though he and his people had suffered much at the hands of the English. His son Alexander was known as the flower of courtiership, and he proved to be a wise ruler in war and in peace. It was he who took Roxburgh Castle in later years and held it for a long time, till a plot hatched by traitors killed him. Wallace was delighted to have Sir John on his side and with him in person. Also among them was a prelate by the name of St Clair, nobly born, and who later became Bishop of Dunkeld till the English drove him into refuge with James the Lord Steward. And on the fifth day of the council they were joined by the small army left behind on the march. They had found plenty of armour and gear on the field of slaughter where MacFadyan met his fate, and helped themselves to it. Wallace made them right welcome. Once the council ended, Wallace set off with his army in the direction of Perth – then known as St Johnston.

Wallace Takes Perth

Wallace conferred with Sir John Ramsay on the possibility of taking Perth. He was eager for revenge for the disaster he had suffered there when he lost all his men.

Ramsay said that Perth was hard to defend because, though the moat was deep, the walls low, and with so many men, it would be easy to fill up a part of the moat so that the men could cross in big numbers. Wallace was cheered and they rode happily on to Dunkeld, where they lodged for a few days while the ordnance was prepared for the assault. Ramsay got the best wrights of the district to make strong wooden frames which were used to help fill the moat, and as earth and stones were added they soon had a broad road across it, surfaced with planks and hurdles. Then with their ladders and equipment for scaling walls, the army surged across and began the assault. The Graham and Ramsay besieged the turret bridge while Wallace led a party against the central gate. The English made a stout defence with their artillery of arblast guns and stones, slings, crossbows and the like. The battle was fierce at the walls but the overwhelming force of the Scots was too much for them and soon a thousand men were over the walls and into the town. Panic seized the town's people and soon there was a great hullabaloo of shouting men and screaming women. The Graham and Ramsay had a hard time at the turret, but they were soon reinforced by a loyal squire, Ruthven by name, and his men, and the turret was taken. It is said about two thousand Englishmen died that night and the streets ran with blood. Sir John Stewart and sixty men escaped in a barge down the Tay to Dundee. Wallace stayed for four days in Perth and all the English were put to the sword. There was plenty of gold, jewellery and other valuables in the town, and this was all taken by the Scots. Wallace made Ruthven captain and filled the town with native Scots to replace the English invaders. Then, leaving the good Ruthven as Sheriff of the town, Wallace and his men headed north to Aberdeen where he held another council. Then he rode to Coupar Angus and visited the Abbey, which the English bishop had deserted.

After a night in Brechin they rode out again, displaying the banner of Scotland for all to see and many of the nobility were with him.

The Destruction of the English at Dunnotar

The Scots rode proudly through the Mearns in battle array behind their banner. The English fled before them to Dunnotar on the coast, hoping to escape by sea. As there were no ships for them they formed up desperately in defence. They tried to get the bishop of the Kirk there to appeal to Wallace on their behalf, and meantime took refuge in the Kirk hoping that might save them from Wallace's vengeance. But Wallace had had enough English treachery. He ordered the Kirk to be set on fire and those who did not die in the fire died in the sea or on the cliffs trying to escape. The more religious of the Scots were appalled by this; to them, it was an act of sacrilege and they knelt before the bishop begging for absolution of their guilt in the business. But Wallace jeered at them, saying, 'Have you forgotten what they did to our true nobles in Ayr? I'll give you all the absolution you need.'

A Hundred Ships Burned

Wallace now marched back to Aberdeen where he found the English garrison loading up on a hundred ships in the harbour, making their escape to England. The Scots swooped at once, slaying every man they could get their hands on. Then they seized the ships, looted them of their gear and burned them. Only the priests, women and children were spared in that massacre. Wallace then rode on to Buchan Castle where Lord Beaumont was in charge. He had recently been made an earl, but when he heard that Wallace was approaching he fled from the castle and boarded a ship from Slains for England. Wallace rode about through the north country slaying every Englishman of arms-bearing age he could find. The Scots now flocked to his banner, though the nobles held back because of their lands in England and because Wallace was a commoner and their social inferior. It was with a happy band of warriors he spent Lammas that year in Aberdeen.

The Siege of Dundee Castle

Wallace decided to take Dundee Castle next and laid siege to it with his troops. Meanwhile Sir Aylmer de Valence, that vile traitor, finding Scotland too dangerous now, fled to England with his household, forsaking his lands and depending on Edward's charity. In order to excuse himself, he exaggerated Wallace's achievements in Scotland, blowing him up larger than life. Great was the lamentation in England over the lost kinsfolk who had perished in Scotland, not to mention wealth and gear. Edward was too preoccupied with France at the time to do anything about Scotland, so he sent Lord Cressingham, his treasurer, and the Earl of Warren with an army instead. They were ordered to hold Stirling until the king himself was able to come and put down the Scots once and for all. Full of confidence, they arrived at Berwick where they were welcomed by the traitor Patrick, Earl of Dunbar. He still held the castle of Dunbar and from there he worked as much mischief on behalf of the English and against his fellow-Scots as he could. Then they marched on for Stirling, a huge army said to number about sixty thousand. When they arrived at Stirling they besieged the castle held by Earl Malcolm, who was in great danger. Word was sent to Wallace and he left one of his trusted captains to keep up the siege of Dundee with two thousand men while he and the others made at once for Stirling to relieve Earl Malcolm. They passed by Perth and set up camp in Sheriffmuir.

The Battle of Stirling Brig

Wallace conferred with Graham and Ramsay and other trusty leaders about how best to deal with Stirling. To meet the English in open combat, so few against so many, would have been idiotic. Yet they had to beat them somehow. But how? It so happened that the English army in order to reach the castle had to cross the narrow bridge over the Forth. Wallace decided to meet the English on the far side of the bridge when a certain number had crossed over. He ordered a wright to saw through the main beams of the bridge in the middle, then give them a temporary mend with a pin which could be pulled out at a given signal, causing the bridge to collapse. The wright himself was hidden in the superstructure of the bridge and he was told to pull the pin out when Wallace blew his horn. The Scots drew up in battle formation a few hundred yards from the far side of the bridge, leaving enough room for more than their own number of English. The English army outnumbered the Scots by about six to one, and their leaders were the Earl of Cressingham and the Earl of Warren, as we have seen. Cressingham took the van with many thousands of men and an awesome spectacle they were as they approached the bridge on that day, 11 September 1297. The Earl of Warren led the second army due to follow Cressingham and his. Quite unsuspecting, Cressingham rode onto the bridge, his men following four abreast, the most it could take. Wallace sat intently on his horse till the Cressingham army was almost all across, then sounded his horn. The wright pulled out the pin and the bridge collapsed, throwing scores of men and horses in heavy armour into the Forth, where they were drowned. Warren was cut off by the broad river, unable to help the first army now on the other side. Then Wallace and his men charged the English. The Scots were outnumbered but fought with the ferocity of men defending their own firesides whereas the English had no such morale to boost them, and what morale they had was undermined by perception of the trap they had been led into. Soon the fight became a massacre, Graham, Boyd, Ramsay, Lundy and Murray especially distinguishing themselves. Wallace was able to pick out Cressingham by the high plumes flaunting above his helmet and hammered his way through to him. He soon got within range and charged with couched spear. The point took the knight in the middle of his bright corslet and shore through steel and bone. Cressingham was dead before he hit the ground. This blow thoroughly demoralised the already frightened English and they now sought to flee the field, many trying to swim back across the Forth where they drowned. It is said as many as ten thousand Englishmen were slain that day, and the Scots victory was marred only by the death in battle of Sir Andrew Murray. The rest of the English army south of the bridge fled, like fire from flint, not stopping till they reached Dunbar. The good wright John, who had made the victory possible by his skill and daring, was rescued from his eyrie in the bridge, then Wallace and his men set off in pursuit of the fleeing English. Having nothing more to fear, Earl Malcolm sallied out of the castle with a troop of Lennox men and joined the chase. They caught up with stragglers in the rear of the fleeing English and slew them, and as the horses tired on the journey, the numbers who thus fell to the Scots increased to a large number. Earl Warren himself by changing horses on the way reached Dunbar with Corspatrick and others. Many of the Scots horses also tired so that both armies thinned out.

Wallace and the Graham kept close together and made a great slaughter of English stragglers at Haddington. There Wallace deemed it useless to pursue further and let the two English captains escape to Dunbar. The Scots stayed that night in Haddington and made their way back to Stirling next day. It was one of the greatest victories in Scottish history, surpassed only by Bannockburn in later years, and even the nobles began to flock to Wallace and the cause of Scotland. Wallace welcomed all who came in good will, whatever their past had been.

Menteith Takes the Oath

Among these nobles was Sir John Menteith, Lord of Arran. In front of witnesses he swore loyalty to Wallace and the cause of the Scottish kingdom. Those who held out against Wallace and clung to Edward were regarded as traitors and if caught were imprisoned or slain. The English captains still holding Scottish castles now deserted them and fled, except those in Berwick and Roxburgh. Dundee was surrendered in return for the lives of the garrison, who were allowed to escape by sea to England. Most of the English who got to Dunbar escaped thence into England but one, an English captain called Harbottle who had held Jedwood Castle, was intercepted with his men by a worthy Scots baron called Chrystal of Seaton and slain in the ensuing fight. Chrystal went on to take Jedwood Castle with much wealth and gear left by the English. Ruthven was left in charge of Jedwood Castle, subject to Wallace's approval. Chrystal later distinguished himself in Bruce's war of independence.

The noble Wallace was now at the height of his power and a worthy governor he proved to be. He chose wise and worthy men to be sheriffs and captains, mostly from his own kindred and comrades whose worth had been proven in the long and bitter struggle. His own cousin Crawford, for instance, was made Keeper of Edinburgh Castle, with many good adjutants under him. Scotland, which had endured such harrowing sorrows and trials, was now free again under its great liberator and Governor, the heroic Wallace. But the problem of the kingship still remained, for Wallace had no legal or moral claim to the crown, nor ever entertained such ambition. Yet without a proper king restored to the kingdom the rule of Wallace was a temporary, shaky rule. Robert Bruce, whom Wallace looked to as king in Baliol's default, was still in England, a virtual captive, it is said, of King Edward, who watched him constantly.

Chapter 8

This happy time for Scotland lasted five months, during which Wallace called a council of the Three Estates in Perth. It was important that as many of the nobles as possible attended to take part in governing Scotland according to its constitution. One of these nobles was the traitor Earl Corspatrick of Dunbar and Wallace got the parliament to invite him, promising him a pardon if he now swore loyalty to the crown of Scotland. But Corspatrick refused to come and jeered at Wallace, a mere commoner, as the 'King of Kyle'. He jeered at Wallace's Guardianship, saying he, Corspatrick, held no land from the 'King of Kyle' but was a free lord of his own domains in Scotland and in England. The jibe about the kingship, which Wallace never in any way sought, made Wallace particularly angry. He proposed to the assembled parliament that this rebel lord be brought to heel and made to acknowledge his fealty to the crown of Scotland. He would rue the day he sent such an insolent reply to the Three Estates of the Realm of Scotland. The Estates agreed, and Wallace prepared to attack Dunbar in order to bring Corspatrick back by force to swear allegiance. He took two hundred men with him, leaving the Council to carry on without him.

Once over the Forth they hastened through Edinburgh to Musselburgh where Robert Lauder, a faithful Scot who kept clear of Edward's entangling net, met them with his men, intent to ride with them against Dunbar. Chrystal of Seton also joined them so that there were four hundred men in all by the time they approached Dunbar. At Linton they were met by a squire of the district called Lyall who told them that Corspatrick was then at Cockburnspath. He advised Wallace to ride straight for Dunbar which would be easily taken in the Earl's absence, then they could await his return. Wallace, who thought Corspatrick so able a knight that he wanted to win him over, was doubtful of this and indeed they soon heard that the Earl was waiting for them with about nine hundred men at a field of his own choosing near Innerwick. There was no one there with the authority to try to bring Wallace and Corspatrick to a parley and perhaps peaceful agreement, so both sides simply charged at once. It was a hard-fought battle from which, after much slaughter of his men, Earl Corspatrick fled back to Cockburnspath with a handful of his men. Wallace lost no time in making for Dunbar where he easily took the castle. He found it almost bare of provisions and gear for the Earl had taken all that could be carried. Wallace set Chrystal of Seton in charge, and that worthy man soon filled it with provender, gear and men to defend it. Next day Wallace set out with three hundred men to attack Corspatrick at Cockburnspath. Corspatrick's scouts warned him of the coming attack and, rather than face it, the traitor fled to Bonkill Wood, and from there to Norham. Wallace followed as far as Coldstream and stayed there for the night. Corspatrick disappeared into the forest where it was difficult for Wallace effectively to follow and take him, and he escaped down into England for help. Wallace also sought reinforcements and made for the west country. Corspatrick met up with Bishop Beck in his ride south and told him the news. Beck of course, having been driven out of Glasgow when Wallace had slain the Percy, had his own reasons for wanting revenge on Wallace.

Beck and Bruce Invade Scotland

Bishop Beck raised a large army in Northumberland ready to march on Wallace. Bruce, who was in the area, had been persuaded by Edward's lies that Wallace, a mere commoner, in fact sought the crown of Scotland for himself and not for its rightful king. He therefore decided to join Beck and win the crown of Scotland for himself, regarding Wallace as a rebel and usurper. So the man for whom Wallace sought the crown in fact was deceived into believing that loyal hero, his best friend, to be his enemy. They marched north and set up camp at Norham. Meanwhile Corspatrick marched with an army to Dunbar where he laid siege to the castle. Ships were sent from Newcastle to blockade Dunbar harbour, preventing supply ships from entering or leaving. Wallace had managed to raise an army of some five thousand men and now set out for Dunbar to help Seton and raise the siege. At Yester he was met by Hay and his fifty well-armed men and informed of Corspatrick's strength. Wallace resolved to press on to the attack, not knowing of Beck's army lying in wait at Norham.

Corspatrick now laid a trap for Wallace. He decided to meet Wallace with all his strength outside Dunbar at a place called Spot Muir. He sent word to Beck and Bruce of his intention and told them to approach from a direction which would take Wallace unawares from the side, if not indeed in time to ambush him. When Seton saw the Corspatrick army in the field he sallied out with some of his best men, leaving the rest to defend the castle, intent on helping Wallace. Some of Wallace's comrades, when they saw the strength of Corspatrick's army advised against fighting a pitched battle against such odds. Not knowing of Beck's hidden army, Wallace refused the advice saying one of his men was worth four of the others, and charged. The ensuing battle was ferocious, the loyal Scots fighting like tigers at bay. Corspatrick himself was a warrior of the best and but for his own example his men would have broken before they did. As it was, after some heavy fighting and heavier losses, Corspatrick's men began to give way and flee, but at that moment Beck's army came on to reinforce them.

Wallace was utterly shocked and pained to see the Bruce's standard flown against his own people. It was a blow no other could have struck against him. He thought of ordering his men off the field, then realised it was almost impossible to do anything now but fight on. That day, Bruce slew many of his own people, as did the traitor Corspatrick and Bishop Beck. Wallace sought to get through to the Earl himself but was prevented by one Maitland, whom he slew. Corspatrick's sword caught Wallace on the thigh, wounding him, but before Wallace could get back at him the press of men separated them. Wallace soon found himself isolated from his own men and surrounded by foes. His mighty sword kept a clearance round him, but Corspatrick ordered his spearmen to bring him down, but the great sword shore the head off any spear that came near him. The Scots soon noticed Wallace was isolated and sought to aid him, Graham, Lauder, Lyall and Hay chief among them, with Lundy, Boyd and Seton. Beck was knocked from his horse in this melee, and before he got to his feet Wallace had been rescued from his tight corner. Now hopelessly outnumbered, Wallace ordered a retreat, and they escaped to the forest where Corspatrick and the others would find it difficult to follow. Beck and his army camped that night in the Lammermuirs, Corspatrick fuming and fretting at his bad luck. Beck feared that Wallace, whose worth against overwhelming odds had been proven that day, would lose no time in gathering reinforcements and return for revenge. In this he was right, for the powerful

Crawford rode in from Edinburgh with three hundred mounted men, while others flocked in from Teviotdale, Ruthven from Jedwood, and Sir William with eighty men. By nightfall about two thousand fresh troops had joined Wallace, whose scouts brought news of the whereabouts of Beck and Corspatrick. As soon as supper was over, Wallace marched his men over to the Lammermuirs ready for next day and they spent the night near their enemies. Wallace had divided his men into two companies, one under Graham helped by Seton, Lauder and Hay, the other under his own command with Lundy, Ramsay, Douglas, Barclay, Boyd, and Adam Wallace.

When the sun rose, the two armies were in sight of each other, the English taken by surprise. While they were still unprepared, Wallace charged at once, working furious havoc on them. Graham and his men soon came up on the flank and the English were caught in a pincer movement. Many of the English fled after a few minutes of the onslaught leaving only a hard core round Beck, who was defended by an English knight called Skelton. Lundy got through to this man and after a few exchanges caught him such a stroke on the neck that he shore through both steel and bone. Seeing this great champion cut down so demoralised the English that they fled, Beck, Corspatrick and Bruce fleeing with them. They rode as fast as they could for Norham Castle, and the Scots pursued them, slaying all they could catch up with, and many were drowned trying to cross the Tweed. Thus the young Lord Robert Bruce, future victor of Bannockburn, was put to shame and ignominious flight by William Wallace, the man who so suffered in his cause and that of Scotland. But Wallace was sore at heart for Bruce, for he'd rather have had him on his side than all the gold the Greeks found in Troy. God, what they might have done together!

Once again Corspatrick had escaped his just deserts, but his lands remained, and Wallace rode through them with fire and sword, laying waste all that might have benefitted the traitor. The seven huge provision houses known as Meathouses were raided and then razed to the ground, and after two weeks only Dunbar Castle was left standing. Wallace then marched first to Glasgow then on to Perth, where he appraised the Council of how he had tried to bring the rebel earl to Perth, but having failed, had confirmed Corspatrick's statement that he owed no land in Scotland. He was now a poor dependant on his master Edward's charity. The Scots lords thanked God for William Wallace and his achievements, and in their gratitude made Wallace Governor of the whole of Scotland.

It was only right that Wallace should now reward all those loyal men who had served with him so valiantly in Scotland's cause and Lauder, Lyall, Scrymgeour and many others were given lands. He gave no land to his own kinsmen, being too scrupulous, but he did give them office instead. And to rub in the lesson of his own integrity and lack of selfseeking, he refused any reward unless and until it should be the pleasure of the rightful king of Scotland restored to his throne. So much for Bruce's fear that Wallace aimed at the Crown.

For a time peace returned to the land and Scotland was better off than at any time since the death of King Alexander in 1286.

The Invasion of England

Meantime Corspatrick gave his lord and master Edward so lurid a story of Wallace's exploits in Scotland that Edward was enraged beyond even his choleric wont, and swore that he himself would lead an army to crush Wallace and the Scots. News of this reached Wallace through his spies and he gathered all his army on Roslyn

Moor. There he told them the news and that rather than wait for Edward he intended to give the English a taste of their own medicine by laying waste the north of England as they had done to Scotland. Let the fighting be done on English soil for a change. He exonerated all the great lords from accompanying him if they preferred to stay in Scotland: but they, commoner though he was, all said they would march with him. With such backing, Wallace had about twenty thousand men when the army marched south from Roslyn Moor. Earl Malcolm refused any command but kept close to Wallace as adviser and bodyguard, and this pleased Wallace, for the Earl was as wise as he was strong. Campbell, Ramsay, Graham, all the loyal comrades rode with him, and a regal army they were.

The first goal was Roxburgh, and Wallace himself rode ahead with only forty men, right up to the castle gate. The English in the castle were amazed at his daring, especially when he forthrightly requested a parley with the commander, Sir Ralph Gray. That knight came to the wall above the gate and Wallace told him, 'I have no time to waste at present to besiege you here. We are going into England to repay them for some of the crimes they have committed in Scotland and when I come back I expect you to be ready to hand over the keys of the castle to me. If you don't, I will take the place by force of arms and hang you from the flagstaff.' Thus saying, he rode back to join his army. Wallace then sent Ramsay to deliver a similar ultimatum to the English in Berwick.

The Scots army then crossed the Tweed into England and began to harry the whole Northumbrian countryside, sparing no man of military age and laying waste the land. They swept all before them right down to Durham which they put to the fire. Everywhere they went they spared the abbeys and churches. They went down as far as York, burning and slaying all the way. They took no lords for ransom, despising such wretched bargaining, but slew all regardless of rank. Incensed at this outrage, King Edward sent messengers to Wallace, a knight, a squire and a cleric, saying if Wallace would stop this merciless slaughter forthwith he gave his word to meet him in open battle within forty days. He also said, 'As you have freed so much of Scotland, why not be content and leave England alone.' Wallace heard them out, then told them that he was only doing his duty by Scotland, threatened by Edward, making his march north that much more difficult and doing to England what the English had done many times to Scotland. But he conceded that if Edward would meet him in battle he would indeed grant a truce for the required forty days, though setting no trust in any truce made by Edward. The truce signed and sealed, the messengers returned to Edward, saying what a grim lot the Scots army was. Edward agreed that it would be foolish to underrate a man like Wallace with his fanatical purpose and army.

Meanwhile Wallace marched north-west to Northallerton and camped there to await the English. A certain Sir Ralph Raymond who was commander of Maltoun decided to try to ambush Wallace with a large army by springing a surprise attack on him, but Wallace was forewarned by his spies in the district. Wallace decided to turn the tables and taking a force of his best men chose a spot the English must pass and lay in ambush. The English were taken completely by surprise as the Scots rushed out on them. Wallace, as usual, aimed at the leader and slew Sir Ralph with a spear. As soon as they knew their leader was dead, the English morale plummeted and they began to desert the field. This was not so easy, however, and it is said about three thousand of them were slain in that encounter. The Scots then took the town and pillaged it of all the gear and provender they could find, which was much. Three days they stayed there, then sending the women and children out of it, they razed it to the ground. With the rubble, the Scots built themselves a wall of defence against attack from the south.

Edward had promised to meet Wallace in battle, but the English barons objected to this because Wallace was a commoner and it was beneath the dignity of their king to treat such a man as if he were a king or a great lord. The parliament decided that unless Wallace were crowned king of Scots it was beneath them to meet him in open battle. Moreover, if Edward won the battle, he had gained little but perhaps the retreat of the Scots to Scotland: but if he lost it, the Scots would materially have power over all England. We therefore have the curious spectacle of the English king and barons asking that Wallace be crowned king so that Edward could then fight him and try to reduce him to a vassal to himself. One can imagine Wallace's amused reaction when word was brought to him of this. But it was a serious temptation to treason against the crown of Scotland and Wallace had to take it seriously because many of his friends counselled him to take the crown: they wanted the battle. Wallace therefore made a proclamation that in no circumstances would he so rebel against the lawful king of Scots, whoever that may be (and Bruce now had the prior claim), on whose behalf as a loyal subject Wallace fought his campaigns. And besides, as he pointed out, only the Scots parliament still in Scotland could take any such step: it was completely out of his hands and he would be a usurper if he took it upon himself. He was then counselled by some to take the crown only nominally for a day, so that the battle might be fought. This Wallace also refused, laughing, and saying, 'You can put it about if you like, start a rumour, but I myself refuse to do anything so dishonourable as take the Crown of Scotland on myself for even a day, no matter what advantage the cause might gain thereby.' The two knights who had come as emissaries were therefore not allowed to see Wallace himself but were told the lie that he had indeed been crowned.

The knights went back to Edward with the news, which was received with mixed reactions, some saying that Wallace was bad enough as a mere commoner but now that he was king he would be quite impossible. These men were against giving battle, others said it could not now be avoided. Unable to decide, they simply did nothing. This in fact became something of a policy, for they hoped that lack of provisions would soon tire the Scots of any further ravaging in England and make them turn home. To this end it was ordered that no markets in England were to sell anything to or that might reach the Scots: this affected the whole of the north from Trent to Tweed.

Wallace waited the forty days of his word and five more, but Edward never came against him. Wallace therefore denounced Edward as a liar and coward, no man of his word and so worthy of no respect. And in front of his army he threw down Edward's seal and trampled it into the ground, raising his own banner on high. The raids were resumed throughout Yorkshire, sparing only priests and women and children, until they came to York itself.

Wallace Besieges York

Arriving at the walls of York, the Scots at once began to lay siege to it. The army was divided into four parts and surrounded the town in every direction, setting watches to ensure that none could enter or leave the town. Wallace took the south area with Lundy second in command; Earl Malcolm took the west with Boyd; Campbell of Lochawe took the north with Ramsay and Sir John the Graham with Auchinleck (Affleck) and Crawford took the east. The Scots had a thousand archers, but the English had several times that number inside the town. An assault was made at once on the walls. It was a fierce contest, the Scots shooting fiery arrows into the town to start fires among the houses, with marked success. The English replied with catapulted stones and boulders, with archery and fiery bundles of sticks and cauldrons of burning tar and the like. By nightfall the Scots had done much damage to the walls and the town. They laid off for the night but still ringed the town and posted sentries to keep the townsfolk in. Apart from a few wounds, bruises and burns they had suffered almost no casualties.

Next day they rose with the sun and again assailed the town, their deadly arrows taking toll of the defenders. But despite near success in burning some of the gates, the resistance was so stubborn that the second day ended as the first, with the English still in command of the town. Once more the Scots settled down for the night outside the walls. Meanwhile, the English decided to make a surprise sally out of the town to attack the sleeping Scots, led by Sir John Norton and Sir William Lees. With five thousand men, it is said, they poured out of the west gate and attacked Earl Malcolm and his men. It chanced that Wallace had been riding round the Scots and was approaching Earl Malcolm's troops when he saw this sally. He at once sounded the alarm thus giving the Scots time to rise and arm, those indeed who were not sleeping fully armed. Wallace and his troop hurled themselves into the fight and, having lost the element of surprise they had banked on, the English got a hot reception. It is said that no knight since King Arthur matched Wallace in feats of arms and so it was proved that night. Sir John Norton fell never to rise, and some twelve hundred more: the rest of the English fled back to the town. Next day they mounted the attack again, but still could make no breach in the stout defence. By this time, the Scots provisions were running low, as were those of the town, and unaware of the plight of the Scots, the English began to talk of treating with Wallace, and eventually the mayor sent word to Wallace asking to parley with him. Wallace came to hear his offer of gold and gear if he would lift the siege and ride on to other towns. They could not endure the shame of yielding so big a town as York. Wallace replied that he cared nothing for gold and gear but wanted battle, which the king had promised him. Failing that, he wanted revenge. The mayor replied that he could not answer for the king but repeated his offer of ransom. The Scots held a council of war and the majority opinion was that as it would take too long to capture the town they should content themselves with the ransom money. Wallace was reluctant to accept the majority opinion but agreed on condition that the English should also set up the Scottish flag on their battlements for a stated number of hours. The English agreed to this, it was done, the ransom paid, and the siege lifted.

As provision was now scarce in the ravished north the Scots began their raids again, driving further south till even London was alarmed and begged the king to do something about it. The whole of the Midlands were pillaged by the raiding Scots. It is even said that some threatened to go over to Wallace if the king would not protect them against him. But Edward made no move to give battle to Wallace, who went rampaging on as before.

There was a rumour that Edward's queen herself had secret audience of Wallace to try to relieve her harassed subjects and achieve a truce, and that as a result the English promised to give up Roxburgh and Berwick to the Scots, and to send Wallace certain Scots nobles then in London with the king. Among these were Comyn and de Soulis, but Bruce was in Calais and the traitor de Valence fled to Picardy lest he be turned over to Wallace. The Earl

Patrick was also among those returned and, swearing fealty to the Scottish crown, was forgiven and restored by Wallace. With this and Roxburgh and Berwick again in Scots hands, Wallace decided to call it a day and the army turned north for Scotland. Wallace sent emissaries to Bruce asking him to come and take the Scottish crown as rightful king, but Edward had poisoned Bruce against Wallace.

With Scotland now at peace again, Wallace left it in good hands and went on a visit to the continent, particularly to France, where he stayed a while at the French court and even, it is said, met the deposed ex-king of Scots John Baliol in exile there.

Chapter 9

Wallace Encounters the Red Reiver

Wallace left Scotland for the continent as secretly as was possible. If word had got to the English, for instance, they would have used their navy to intercept the ship and capture him. Also, as many of the Three Estates would have objected to his going at all, only a few close to Wallace were told of his plan. He took only fifty men with him, his own kinsmen among them, Crawford, Kneland and some more of his most trusted friends and lieutenants. They deemed it safer to sail the east coast route, and a ship was prepared and victualled at Kirkcudbright, crewed with hand-picked seamen. On the appointed day Wallace and his men were rowed out to the ship, she upped anchor and set sail from Scotland with a good breeze behind her.

On the second day out, the captain spied a ship with sixteen red sails which put him in considerable alarm. It was moving towards them from the south-east horizon. The captain knew that a most dreaded pirate was bearing down on them. In great alarm he informed Wallace, regretting he had ever taken the responsibility of the safety of the Guardian upon himself. The pirate was known as the Red Reiver, a tyrant who spared no one from the ships he looted, whether king or commoner. He had terrorised the seas for sixteen years and was an invincible sea-warrior. Wallace enquired about the man, and the captain described him and how he himself was always the first man to board a victim ship, dressed in red, with a coat of arms on his chest. Wallace sent the captain below and called his own fifty men on deck. There he made his plans to meet the scourge of the waves, keeping most of his men hidden and only Crawford, a skilled sailor, ready to strike sail when ordered. Kneland took over the helm and Wallace himself stood by to intercept the pirate.

The pirate ship drew near enough for its bloodthirsty crew of pirates to be seen, the Reiver himself standing on the gun'le ready to leap aboard the Scots boat, calling aloud to it to surrender or die. Crawford slacked sail a bit as the pirate came alongside. The Reiver fearlessly leapt aboard, only to find himself in the mighty grip of William Wallace who seized him by the throat and hurled him down on the deck. Crawford deftly swung the wheel so that the gap widened between the two boats before any of the others could join their master or fix grappling irons. The Reiver lay on the deck with Wallace's dagger at his throat. He gasped out a plea for his life. Wallace, who never yet spared an enemy of English nationality, spared this man, partly because he was French and partly because there was still danger from the pirate ship which was now loosing off with a cannon. He told the Reiver he would spare his life if he called off his men and made peace with the Scots. This the Reiver was glad to do, signalling to his men and proffering his glove to Wallace in token of surrender. Then Wallace made him swear never again to take arms against the Scots. Thus a truce was made with this formidable pirate and the Scots had him as escort, in case of English interception, all the way to Rochelle. The Reiver told Wallace his story, how he had fallen foul of the king of France and as a result was forced into his present marauding way of life. For sixteen years he had made himself a kingdom on the sea and spared none of French nationality who fell into his hands, so angry he was with the king who had wronged him and murdered his kinsmen. He had never before met a man who equalled, let alone bested him, and out of his awe at his mighty captor grew a friendship between the two. The Reiver's name was Thomas de Longville and when he realised who Wallace was, having heard of his great exploits, he was no longer surprised but moved to admiration. Wallace offered to try to obtain a pardon for Thomas from the French king when they met, but while Thomas thanked him he said that thereafter he would only serve Wallace. Thus the friendship grew between them and they and the two crews celebrated it in wine as soon as they were safely into Rochelle, where the sight of the Red Reiver's flag at first caused such panic that ships fled before them. But the red lion of Scotland flown by the Scots ship gave them heart again.

Wallace stayed four days at Rochelle and by his influence made peace between the townsfolk and the red navy of his new friend. He ordered the Red Reiver's crew to guard the coast while their master went with the Scots to Paris where Wallace hoped to get him the king's pardon. He also told them that their days of lawlessness were over and that they must become law-abiding citizens. The Reiver himself disguised himself as one of the Scots attendant on Wallace.

Wallace in Paris

Wallace wasted no time getting to Paris and scouts went forward to inform the king of his coming. The king was eager to meet his great Scottish ally against the English, and decided to meet the Scots in a certain garden of the palace. Fifty-two Scots marched into that place, a most impressive band of hardy warriors, and there knelt in honour of the king. Wallace then rose and made a speech in Latin which impressed even the most cultured of the highly civilised court with its courtly eloquence. The French queen had heard much of this renowned Scots warrior and had sought the king's permission to attend the reception with her ladies. We may imagine the impression the young Scots giant and his men made on these cultured flowers of France. The meeting was a great success, as was the banquet in their honour which followed. After the meal Wallace and the king withdrew with a few of the king's closest advisers to the parlour, and there they discussed many matters of common interest to Scotland and France. They spoke mainly of military affairs, but the king also spoke of the dangers Wallace had faced at sea, especially from pirates. Indeed, he reproached Wallace for not letting him know of his voyage in advance so that units of the French navy could have been sent to escort him. Wallace made light of the dangers, affirming his own self-confidence, but the king went on to say that Wallace did not know how lucky he was, and spoke of the Red Reiver, against whom he swore dire vengeance. That same man, standing by and hearing this, was more than a little uncomfortable. Wallace mischievously asked the king if he would know this terror of the seas if he saw him. The king said it had been many years since he set eyes on him but he might indeed recognize him. So Wallace asked if any of his retainers present resembled him. The king looked keenly at each of the Scots till his eyes fell on the Reiver himself standing beside Wallace. 'Yes,' said the king, 'that tall fellow standing beside you reminds me very much of him.' Wallace then sank down on one knee before the king and reminded him of the great service the Scots had been to France in their battle against the English yoke, how much France owed the Scots in general and himself in particular. The king entirely agreed, and promised to give Wallace a reward, asking him to name what he would like, be it goods, land, gold or whatever. This was the moment Wallace had been waiting for, and he now declared he wanted no material reward at all, but pardon for the tall man by his side. Then he told the king his story and the happy outcome, of his friendship with de Longville, and how France would benefit from the end of his piracy and gain a valuable subject. The king was astonished and sat thinking for a time. Then he saw good reason in Wallace's request, how a fierce enemy could be made a valuable friend. He then made de Longville kneel before him, formally forgave him his crimes and received him back into his peace. The grateful de Longville kissed the king's hand. In this mood of happy reconciliation the king also forgave all the Reiver's fifteen hundred men. In addition, the king made de Longville a knight, and told Wallace that he had thus achieved what money could not have bought.

Thus the great warrior proved himself no less astonishing in the role of peacemaker.

Wallace in Guienne

The Scots stayed in Paris for about a month of peaceful leisure till they began to tire of it and grow restless. Men of action need action, they grow stale in peace and leisure. Now it happened that at that time the English, who had the same designs on France as they had on Scotland and Wales, occupied the French district of Guienne. Wallace now sought leave of the French king to mount an attack, aided by de Longville, against Guienne. Being unused to French troops and the French language, Wallace preferred that he and his nine hundred Scots should make the attack unaided. The whole district was raided with fire and sword, fortresses broken down, and every Englishman who came into their power was slain at once.

There was a town in Guienne called Shenon which the English had captured and occupied. Wallace was keen to discover whether there was any way in which he might retake it and drive the English out. The town stood on a river and was closely surrounded by woods and the Scots crept into this forest one night and lay there till the dawn. Wallace then took four hundred of his best men, leaving the rest under Crawford's command, with instructions to wait in ambush ready to come to the aid of the four hundred. Wallace and his picked force then marched out boldly on the town, flying the great red Lion Rampant of Scotland in the van, plundering outlying suburbs as they went. The flag was not recognized at first, but some of the more experienced English soldiery soon spread the news and, seeing how small the Scots force was, poured out of the town gates to do battle with the raiders, losing many of their number in the earliest encounters: so many indeed that the others fled back to the town. Wallace pressed on toward the woods where the rest of his men lay in ambush, plundering as he went. A much larger and better ordered force of English soldiers now came after them from the town – as many as a thousand, it is said, leaving the town almost unguarded. Close to the woods Wallace turned and made a stand against the pursuing English and Crawford now rushed out with his reinforcements and plunged into the battle. There was great slaughter of the English but many a good Scot also lost his life in the fray. The English fought stubbornly and well but they were now outnumbered by the Scots – a very rare thing indeed. Wallace and his friend de Longville wrought terrible personal slaughter on the enemy and none who crossed with them lived to tell the tale. Overwhelmed, the remaining English fled back to the town. Now it was the Scots who pursued, following hard on the English into the town itself before the gates could be closed. But after the vanguard of the Scots was in, a certain valiant porter managed to drop the portcullis, cutting off the Scots inside, including Wallace, his cousin Richard, Crawford and de Longville. The English now turned and pressed the few Scots hard to the wall, where ferociously they defended themselves. Richard Wallace managed to climb the wall, slay the porter, and pull up the portcullis again, letting the Scots crowd in. Now began great slaughter of the Englishry until the whole town was in Scots hands. All the English soldiers were slain but the women and children were allowed to go together with priests and men too old for war. Wallace was very meticulous about such matters, though merciless to English soldiers. All wealth and gear were confiscated then the town was turned over to the French for reoccupation, and the Scots forged on into other parts of Guienne working havoc among the English.

When the French king heard the good news of Wallace's success he at once got together a force of some twenty thousand men under his brother the Duke of Orleans. They rode into Guienne and joined Wallace, who was now marching on Bordeaux. The English there were preparing to give battle, but when they saw the huge French reinforcements they thought better of it.

News of Wallace's exploits in France soon reached England through such men as the Earl of Gloucester, who held Calais, and there was great debate about it in Parliament. Many claimed that Wallace had broken the truce between Scotland and England but others maintained that this did not involve Scotland as such: Wallace and his men were simply mercenary troops, a common thing at that time. Others said that Wallace had only pledged a truce in Scotland, not in France, and was therefore within the law. But the war faction prevailed and it was decided that Wallace's absence from Scotland made this an ideal time to reinvade it.

Scotland Reinvaded

The new army of invasion was led by the Earl of Gloucester, the Duke of Longcastle and Sir John Siward, who knew the north well. Aylmer de Valence also rode with them and through him a number of Scots strongholds were surrendered without a fight on promise of lenient treatment. Even before most Scots were aware of the new war launched against them, de Valence was back in power in Bothwell. Sir John Siward's contingent went by sea and, sailing up the Tay, they took Dundee and Perth and soon the whole of Fife was under their rule. The whole of the lowland and border areas south of Clyde and Tay were again under the English domination, though some lairds escaped to various western isles, including Adam Wallace, who fled to Rathlin. Sir John Graham hid in the forests of the Clyde Valley. Richard Lundy also went into hiding, but trying to contact the Graham, and after some narrow escapes the two parties, Lundy and Graham and their men, met up south of Tinto. There they pitched camp and heard that a train of wine and provisions was on its way from Carlisle to de Valence in Bothwell. Lundy and the Graham at once decided to attack the train. They lay in wait in a wood above the road it must travel, and when the train which included eighty men came near enough, the fifty Scots dashed down on the cumbrous wagons, fewer in number but well-mounted and armed. The English were taken completely by surprise and it is said that in the ensuing slaughter they lost about three-quarters of their number, but only five Scots were killed. The Scots gained more goods, provisions, horses, gear and gold than they knew what for the time being to do with. The district of course was too dangerous to stay in and, stealing through the forest at night, they made their way north and west to the Lennox. There they found Earl Malcolm in command and they helped him to stay in power.

Seton and Lyle managed to escape to the Bass Rock where they had every chance of holding out, but Hugh Hay was captured by the English and taken prisoner to England. Never had Scotland more needed her inspired leader and word was sent to France telling him of the new invasion and asking him to return at once and take the war in hand. The messengers landed in Holland but pressed on at once into France and then down to Guienne. Wallace was infuriated by this further act of English perfidy, saying that he had thought that as the king's honour was involved they would not break the truce without warning. He swore that never again would he trust the word of the treacherous English king, and he would be avenged.

Leaving Guienne at once Wallace hurried back to take his leave of the French king who was reluctant to let him go: but he realised that Wallace had no choice and, offering him any rank he might covet, and making him promise to return to France when he could, let him go. Sir Thomas de Longville of course also left with his leader Wallace. The messenger's ship, under Guthrie, lay at Sluys and so the Scots sailed for home. They sailed past the rivers Forth and Tay and landed at Munross in the north. From there the word soon spread that the Guardian was home again and men began to flock to him. First to reach him were Sir John Ramsay of Ochterhouse, and Ruthven and Barclay with many well-armed men in attendance. With a small but doughty army Wallace immediately marched south to Perth, where the English were once again in power.

Perth Retaken

Wallace and his army halted at the back of Kinnoull Brae where they considered the situation and planned their attack.

It so happened that certain Englishmen were in the habit of leaving the town with carts to collect loads of hay. Wallace fell upon one such party of six men and three carts and slew the men immediately. Some of the Scots including Wallace and Ruthven then dressed in the clothes of Englishmen. Five or six Scots men of arms were then loaded into each cart and lightly covered with hay, and the party made its way by a short cut to the town. The main Scots army under Ramsay crept after them as close as they dared, ready to storm the gates at the given signal. These braw 'carters' passed over the drawbridge unsuspected and through the gates of the town. There the carts suddenly sprang to life, Wallace slaying the porter immediately. The gates were jammed open, and Ramsay, seeing all this, at once rode to their aid. By the time he got through the gates Wallace and his heroes had already slain sixty of the English who, taken completely by surprise, had little time to prepare themselves for such deadly battle and making prudence the better part of valour they took to their heels and fled the town, leaving it to the triumphant Scots. Many were drowned trying to cross the Tay, or in the moat around the town.

A party of the Scots pursued the fleeing English, sparing only the women and children in their usual way. A hundred men who sought sanctuary in the church were dragged out and put to the sword for their crimes against the Scots. Sir John Siward had been the English captain and he now rode to Fife where he gathered an army with which he hoped to retake Perth. Wallace appointed Ramsay captain of Perth and carried on from there with a chosen party of men to explore Fife and assess the situation there. He did not know at this time how powerful the English were in this region.

Sir John Siward, whose spies informed him of Wallace's approach, came over the Ochils to intercept him, staying the night in Abernethy. Wallace was then at

Black Irnside and next day Siward marched there to meet him with fifteen hundred men. Wallace tried to contact Ramsay in Perth for reinforcements but found Siward had cut off his retreat: the messengers could not get through. Wallace discussed the situation with his leading men, including Bisset, who knew the terrain better than most. They agreed that de Valence and the other Scots traitors were more trouble than the English, which was why the messengers could not get through: the Scots traitors knew the forest too well. Guthrie thought their only chance was to get word to Ramsay somehow, and Wallace even considered swimming the icy River Tay. He dismissed this idea because he could not leave his men and no other man was likely to survive the swim. So Wallace decided to brave it out – they were in a place easily defended by a few against many, and he recalled earlier successes when a handful of Scots in a strong position defeated a far greater number of English. He felt they could hold the place at least until hunger drove them out, and made an invigorating speech to his men to strengthen their hearts for a heroic stand against frightful odds. This had such an inspiring effect on some of the men that they wanted to take to the open field against the enemy, but that of course would have been madness, as their leader pointed out. Instead, he set his men to hew down branches of oak and build them around the hillock they occupied in the form of a round wall, like a palisade or fortress. This was done, making full use of the live trees themselves as central pillars and yet with gaps on two opposite sides from which a sally could be made if need be.

They had no sooner finished this rough defence when the English army came in sight, for this was near the road they had to travel. Siward himself led with a thousand men, having left de Valence with five hundred to patrol the outskirts of the forest. Wallace had forty archers among his men, the rest wielding spear and sword. One of the gaps left in the barrier was spotted by the English vanguard who made straight for it. Wallace used it as a trap to get a few men at a time inside the defence where they were soon slain by the ferocious Scots. Similar havoc was wrought on all who tried to climb the barrier which so operated that those who were able to reach the Scots were outnumbered and slaughtered. Meantime the archers in the trees and branches picked off the horses so that they were either killed or so wounded that they threw their riders and charged wildly about. The English force soon turned into a confused frustrated rabble which finally gave up the attempt and fell back out of the forest to the open field.

Siward was baffled and amazed at their rebuff and rejoined de Valence, asking him what on earth was to be done. That traitor replied, 'We do nothing but leave it to our ally, hunger, who will soon drive them out in search of food. Once we get them in the open they are ours.' But Siward was an idealist and this realistic answer offended his sense of chivalry and knightly honour. He therefore determined to try to win his revenge, and ordered de Valence to take one half of the remaining men and attack one side of the defence while he himself with the rest attacked the other. Wallace seeing the English divide with so obvious a purpose decided on a bold strategy. Some distance down the hillock was another ridge that could be defended by a few against a climbing attacker, and this was the direction Siward had to take. So Wallace left some of his best men inside the defence to cope with de Valence while he took the rest down to the ridge, where they at once began to build a similar barrier of branches. Wallace admired the knightly courage of Siward and wanted to meet it with a similar virtue of his own.

Soon battle commenced, Wallace with Siward at the ridge, Crawford and the others with de Valence at the defence, and once again there was great slaughter. Finding himself baffled again, Siward grew desperate and sought the van and came so far up the ridge he slew one of the Scots defenders. Seeing this, Wallace tried to get to Siward himself but was hampered in the general thrash; but many other Englishmen he slew. At last, finding the task impossible, Siward sounded the retreat. De Valence who, as he had foreseen, had taken a similar mauling at the defence was glad to fall back. His own plan of letting hunger do their work would have saved so many lives he felt quite disgusted by Siward's scrupulousness: starvation may not be the weapon of the perfect knight but it works. The Scots were tired out and in need of rest. Few had been killed but many were wounded and in need of care. Wallace gave thanks to God for their success, and praised Siward: but on de Valence, he swore he would be avenged.

The Scots used the defence enclosure as a sort of field hospital for their wounded. Many of them had lost a lot of blood from serious wounds and many were desperately thirsty, and indeed hungry. Many were likely to die. Wallace grieved over their condition and went off to try to get water, taking a large, deep helmet to carry it in. He found a small burn nearby and quenched his own thirst with clear water that tasted better than wine, filled his helmet, and on his return sent other men to do likewise.

It was now a few hours from sunset and Siward considered no further attempt possible that day – just as well for the Scots. He was now more appreciative of de Valence's original situation and next day, decided to mount a siege on the Scots, surround them, and let hunger do the rest. He therefore proposed to de Valence that he would leave him in charge of the siege force and himself ride to Cupar to raise reinforcements. De Valence at first refused to be left, saying that even if Siward stayed with his men the Scots would still manage to break out before dawn. Siward was enraged and threatened to hang him unless he did what he was told. De Valence, who knew the Scots, went in dread of his life from two sources – Siward and Wallace. A Scots spy who had infiltrated de Valence's men heard the threat from Siward and under cover of dusk stole back to the Scots and told Wallace. There was still enough light for Wallace to make out de Valence among the troops ringing the defence. Wallace saw his advantage and got word to de Valence saying that, as Siward would certainly hang him when he found the Scots gone in the morning, he had best save his skin by joining Wallace. De Valence felt that nothing could stop Wallace winning Scotland again, and accepted the offer. Siward came back to find not only Wallace but de Valence and his men gone. He raged in fury against de Valence and his perfidy to the English king.

Meantime word had reached Ramsay and Ruthven in Perth of how Siward had the Scots at bay. They raised a troop at once and rode to Irnside, where they were met by Wallace and de Valence. Siward was arrayed on the plain challenging open battle and the Scots now had numbers enough to accept the challenge, though still outnumbered by men on the English side. Furious battle commenced at once, the Scots charging the invaders, inflamed by the rightness of their cause while the other side was undermined by being in the wrong. Many English and Scots renegades were slain in the first heat of the battle, Ramsay and Ruthven hammering away in the thick of the fight. Siward himself was surrounded by three hundred of his best men but the van of the English was soon cut to pieces and fled, leaving the hard core around Siward that much more vulnerable. The Scots saw their chance and hemmed the enemy in, hacking at them from all sides: there was no escape possible for Siward. Wallace's advisers suggested he should be taken and held to ransom but Wallace himself refused, saying he had never taken prisoners for ransom and would not begin with Siward.

He therefore put himself in the forefront of battle and soon came face to face with his enemy. Siward stood his ground manfully but was no match for the Scots champion. A sweeping stroke of that mighty sword shore through the neck armour and the spine, almost cutting his head clean off, and Siward fell dead at Wallace's feet. The leader dead, his remaining men were soon slaughtered by the Scots who had lost many good men, including that fine hero Bisset.

Lochleven Castle Recaptured

Ruthven rode back to Perth and Sir John Ramsay went on with his men to take Cupar, while Wallace and the main army stayed at Lindores. With Siward dead there was no more resistance in Fife and the Scots made up for their long fast. De Valence was made their steward and proved an abundant supplier of food and drink. Once they had recovered, they rode on to St Andrews where they quickly hunted the renegade bishop out of town. He and some others escaped by sea to England while Wallace restored the rightful bishop to the see. The whole of Fife was now in Scots hands again except for one place – a stronghold on an island in Lochleven which was still in English hands. Kinghorn was deserted by its English captain who knew he could not stand against Wallace. Wallace camped his men on the shores of Lochleven, and while most of them slept, he took eighteen of his best men and sought out the nearest point to the island with the stronghold. The only boat was tied up on the island itself, so Wallace, having instructed his men, stripped himself and slipped quietly into the cold waters of the loch, his sword tied behind his neck. Stealthily he swam across the stretch of water to the boat and as stealthily untied it and getting it well out from the island slipped aboard and quietly rowed back to his men. There he dried himself and dressed and armed himself, while his men crowded into the boat with drawn swords. Rowing with the utmost care they soon landed quietly on the island and stole up to the door of the hall where the men slept. The door was at once barged in with a beam and the English had no chance: all were slaughtered without mercy, all but the few women and children. Wallace decided the abundant provender on the island might be better consumed on the spot than laboriously ferried over, so he sent word for his main force to come and join him.

The messenger found Ramsay and his men apprehensive for their leader's safety, but they were soon cheered by the message to come and dine with Wallace in Lochleven. They stayed eight days on the island feasting, fishing, enjoying a well-earned holiday. On the eighth day they loaded all moveable gear into the boat and ferried it over. The boat had to make several journeys to get all the men across, but once over the boat was burned and the company set out for Perth. There the good Bishop Sinclair advised Wallace to spend the winter with him at Dunkeld, but Wallace was impatient to clear the English out of Scotland. The bishop said he had too few men as yet for that job and ought at least to try to raise more in the highlands. Wallace agreed with him and appointed Jopp to accompany the bishop to Dunkeld and base a recruitment campaign there. At the same time Blair was sent on a similar mission, in his priest's habit, to the west coast. This meant passing through territory held by the English and the men of the west had the problem of somehow getting past these invaders in order to link up with Wallace. They got as far as the Lennox but there they were held up for a time under Earl Malcolm. Jopp came up against a similar problem in the north, where Comyn, Earl of Buchan, tried to prevent men joining his old rival, of whom he was jealous because Wallace was not a noble but a mere commoner. Nevertheless men did manage to trickle through in small numbers and Blair returned with news that the English in the centre were so confident of victory that the Duke and Earl had left captains to do the job and returned to England. At this good news Wallace took fifty of his best men and marched to Erth Ferry, where the castle was kept by an English captain called Tomlin of Ware.

Erth Recaptured

Tomlin had about a hundred men in his command and they tyrannised the district, among other villainies, forcing a certain Scots fisherman to serve them against his will, by day and night. Wallace sent Jopp out before the dawn to reconnoitre, and he suddenly came upon this fisherman, who was accompanied only by his son. Jopp swiftly drew his knife and seized the man by the throat. He was about to strike when something in the man's eyes and gasps for mercy held his hand. 'You're not English,' said Jopp. 'What are you?' The man explained what had happened to him and begged Jopp to take him to join his own people. So Jopp brought him to Wallace, who made him welcome on hearing his tale. The fisherman had been on the north side of the river with his boat doing a spot of fishing, and the Scots realised that the boat was a godsend to them. They used it to cross over to the south side where the English were, and once ashore burned the boat lest it fall into English hands. They went through the Torwood where Wallace heard news that his uncle was imprisoned by the English and had been forced to give up every bit of gear and wealth he had. Wallace determined to free him as soon as he could.

After a night in the Torwood, where they were fed by a good widow friend of Wallace's, they moved on towards

Erth Castle. The fisherman knew it well and the ditches of foul water which guarded it. Avoiding these, he led them round the back, over a small bridge to a door he knew. The door was unguarded and the Scots simply opened it and, Wallace leading, slipped quietly inside. They made their way on tiptoe to the main hall, and there Wallace boldly stepped in, confronting the messing Englishry. For a moment they were frozen in astonishment at sight of this grim giant before them, then rose in panic as Wallace greeted them with a sardonic salute. Wallace leapt towards Tomlin as his men poured in behind him, the terrible sword shearing through hair and bone, splitting him down to the shoulders. Every one of the hundred men was slain that night of vengeance as the Scots took the castle. A quick search was made for Wallace's uncle, who was found chained in a wet dungeon. Never was uncle so glad to see nephew. The castle was well victualled and they settled in for a night of well-earned feasting, the dead bodies having been thrown into the ditches. Then they set adequate guards on watch and settled down for a night's sleep. Next day they despoiled the place of all valuables, slew some Englishmen who came unsuspecting to the castle, imprisoning the captive women and children meantime in the dungeon lest they warn the English of the situation. The Scots were up and on their way to the Torwood before daybreak, and when they were safe, the women and children were released by a servant.

The Burnings at Dumbarton

Wallace now decided to go to Dumbarton, and on the way was helped by a widow he knew who gave them fodder and money and her nine sons to swell their ranks, hardy men, every one of them. The castle was held by Sir John

Menteith, cursed be his name, a Scots traitor in league with the English invaders. Wallace asked his widow friend to go through the town of Dumbarton, which she knew well, marking all the houses, under cover of darkness, where she knew the English harboured. When this was done, Wallace and his men crept up to the outskirts of the town, where they heard the sound of laughter and boasting. The English soldiers were far gone in their cups, as Wallace and a few of his men drew near the house and listened. The men were boasting what they would do to Wallace and the Graham if they could get their hands on them. Wallace smiled grimly and motioned his men to wait: he then tried the door handle, found it opened, and boldly walked into the place. 'I heard you chaps making merry,' he said, 'and being in need of a drink after a hard sea voyage from Ireland, I couldn't resist coming in. Besides, I want news of this new conquest of Scotland.' 'A drink, is it?' said the English captain roughly. 'I dare say you're one of Wallace's spies, and if so you'll hang for it,' and he motioned to his men to seize Wallace. In a flash the sword was out and in one stroke had split the captain's skull, and almost in the same sweep the point struck a man to the heart. Back to the wall, Wallace took on the other seven but, hearing the noise, Stephen of Ireland burst in followed by Kerlie, and in no time the English were all slain. They forced the host of the house to show them where the main body of the English troops lay in a large house nearby. This was surrounded and set on fire, and all who tried to escape were slain. Then they went round all the other houses and fired them too, killing everyone who escaped the flames.

Having replenished their stores in Dumbarton, the Scots pressed on to Roseneath Castle, also held by the English: Menteith at this time was absent from the district. Wallace learned that the garrison went out to church regularly and laid an ambush at a certain place on their way. It happened that on a certain day a marriage was taking place in the church, and instead of leaving enough men to guard the castle, the whole garrison was to attend, leaving only servants in the castle. During the marriage the Scots took up their position near the castle approach, and as the garrison drew up, suddenly fell on them with such fury that forty were killed in the first attack, about half the total company, and the rest turned tail and fled. The castle was then wide open, and the Scots simply possessed it with little further trouble, Wallace sending a party of horse to pursue and slay the fleeing Englishmen. They stayed seven days at Roseneath living well on the lavish provender there. When they were ready to leave, the walls of the castle were broken down and the place burned and despoiled so that it could never harbour Englishry again. The Scots then rode on to Faslane where Wallace found his uncle Earl Malcolm waiting with such noble Scots as the Graham, Lundy, Adam Wallace, Barclay and Boyd. There too he heard the sad news that his mother had died of an illness in Dunfermline, having had to flee her home in Elderslie for fear of the English. Wallace saw to it that she was buried with full religious honours, but he wasted little time in mourning: her death rather added to his resolve to free their country from the oppressor.

The Castle of Sanquhar Taken

Sir William Douglas, a powerful Border lord, had two sons, James who later became Robert Bruce's right-hand man, and Hugh. The two boys had been sent to France for safety and training. Sir William himself fell into Edward's hands and was kept imprisoned until he agreed to come into the King's peace. His first wife had died years before and to try to keep his loyalty, Edward married him off to a certain Lady Ferrais, daughter of a family of high blood and power in England, but the marriage was not a success. She also bore him two sons, and Edward thought Douglas now safely in his grip. So when Sir William sought permission to return to Scotland with his wife to look after his own lands of Douglasdale, he saw no reason to refuse. But Sir William was an incorruptible Scot and had his own plans. He greatly admired Wallace and believed in the Scottish cause enough to want to contribute to the war of independence. He felt no real debt to Edward into whose service he had been coerced against his will.

It happened that the castle of Sanquhar on the Nith was held by a tyrannical English captain called Beaufort, a kinsman of Douglas's new wife. Douglas thought he might well begin there, and confided in a sturdy young man called Thomas Dickson, who at once promised to help him. Dickson had a cousin called Anderson who was in the habit of supplying wood to the castle and therefore could help them. A plan was agreed and Sir William chose thirty of his best men and rode off, telling his wife he had some English business to settle in Dumfries. They hid that night in a defile by the Craw Water. There Dickson changed clothes with Anderson who was to take a load of wood into the castle first thing in the morning. They learned from Anderson that the garrison consisted of forty men, and he told Dickson that immediately over the drawbridge there was a fine battle-axe kept handy in a neuk on the right hand side of the gate, if he needed it. Dickson took the cart loaded with wood, yoked the horse, and set off toward the castle, Douglas and his men following slowly, led by Anderson. Arriving at the gate, Dickson called on the porter who grumbled at the early hour, but opened up. Once the cart was under the portcullis, Dickson cut the rope that held it up so that if fell on the cart and jammed there. The porter rushed at

Dickson and was slain by the dagger used to cut the rope. Dickson grabbed the axe from its neuk, and Sir William and his men came rushing in as soon as they saw the portcullis stuck in the cart. They moved silently and stealthily, took three watchmen unawares and slew them, and by the time the alarm was raised Sir William had reached the chamber where the captain slept. The captain leapt up and grabbed a sword, but too late – Douglas was in and ran him through the heart. The English were given no time to arm properly, and in no time all but one of them had been put to the sword. One escaped and fled to Durrisdeer and warned the English. Soon the news spread and the English mustered to hunt Douglas and hang him as a traitor. Knowing his danger, Douglas sent word to Wallace while he held the castle of Sanquhar and prepared to meet the coming siege. Wallace at once set off with all his men to help Douglas. He and Earl Malcolm had burned Linlithgow and Dalkeith, then taken refuge at Newbattle for a time, before meeting up with Lauder and Seton and some others who had joined them as they marched through Peebles. They numbered about six hundred against an estimated three thousand of the English all told.

The Siege of Sanquhar

Douglas meantime found himself besieged in the castle, a handful of men against odds of almost a hundred to one. The outcome could only have been the butchery of the Scots, though the English did not know just how few were in the castle. It was a grim outlook, all depending on Wallace arriving in time with enough men to raise the siege. Several days passed, tense and sleepless for the small Scots garrison. But they had an unknown ally outside the walls – cowardice. When word reached the besiegers that

Wallace was approaching with an army, the numbers no doubt exaggerated, fear shook them to the guts. Had not their king himself fled the dreaded Wallace on at least one occasion? The soldiers began to desert and turn tail for England, first in drips and drabs then, as the panic spread, in droves. So it came about that Wallace raised the siege on Sanquhar without giving or taking a single stroke. On hearing the incredible news Wallace felt cheated and decided to pursue the poltroons on their way south, to this end taking three hundred lightly armed men on good horses, leaving Earl Malcolm in command of the others. They rode through Durrisdeer taking the direct road above Morton in case the English tried to hole up in Lochmaben Castle. But they only wished to get out of Scotland as quickly as possible. Wallace overtook them, the main body, and when the English saw so small a force, they felt emboldened to turn and meet it. But Earl Malcolm, coming up more slowly, appeared with what seemed another, larger force, and the English fled. Wallace's men managed to cut off a few score of them and slew the lot, then pressed on after the fleeing force. Riding in among the still fleeing English, they wrought devastating havoc, the more so as they were in no mood to fight. Some five hundred were slain at Dalswinton alone. The Scots horses were now tiring and falling behind, but some fresh ones were brought in and the slaughterous chase went on, three of the English captains among the slain. Wallace drew up at the border, satisfied with the slaughter, and they fell back to Caerlaverock for the night and next day rode happily into Dumfries, where loyal Scots were rewarded and Wallace issued a proclamation to all Scots to join him in the war of liberation, promising an amnesty for all those who had been collaborating with the enemy. He also appointed governors of all towns and castles now abandoned by the retreating English. Sir William Douglas was made warden of all the lands from Drumlanrig to Ayr, having proved his worth at Sanquhar. His wife, however, nursed her hatred of the Scots like a viper in her bosom, biding her time.

Soon the only English commander left in Scotland was Morton at Dundee, and Wallace lost no time in marching there and laying siege to it. Morton saw that his position was hopeless and sought permission to leave safely with his men and return to England. But Wallace had decided to make an example of him and told him that far from letting him go he intended to take him alive and hang him, as a warning to the English of what they could expect if they tried any further invasions of Scotland.

The English managed to get word by ship to King Edward of Morton's dilemma. Edward was at this time in France trying to grab more land from its rightful owners, but when he heard of Wallace's success in Scotland, he was so enraged that he decided to abandon his French adventures, his claim to Gascony in particular, to invade Scotland and destroy Wallace. Once back in England, he began raising an army against the Scots, including all those Scots nobles who because of their lands in England owed him allegiance. One of these was Robert Bruce, Earl of Carrick, who was thus ordered to march against the Scottish hero who was in the process of carving a way to the throne for him, as rightful king of Scots. Edward believed that if he could kill Wallace, the Scots 'rebellion', as he in his insolence called it, would peter out for want of adequate leadership: in which he was largely right, for the only other man of comparable stature and authority was Robert Bruce, then a traitor to his own cause and that of his people.

What was Wallace like? Tradition has it that he was almost seven feet tall, and powerfully built, with massive arms and legs, great shoulders, muscular and athletic, with huge hands, a long handsome face, a mighty chest, a straight nose, brown curly hair and sober of speech. His eyes were grey and piercing, and he had a ruddy complexion, with the scar of a wound on the left side of his neck, and other scars on his body. He was a mild man in peace but a veritable Hector or Achilles in war. He was a good listener to loyal Scots but very suspicious of any whose loyalty he mistrusted, wary of traps, as he had to be. In every way the man was a giant, larger than life, yet simple, frank, and among friends at least, human as well as heroic.

While the siege of Dundee was still going on Wallace got news of the approach of King Edward with an army said to number a hundred thousand. The Scots numbered some ten thousand under arms. Two thousand of these Wallace, whose hopes were dashed by the news, left with Scrymgeour to hold the siege of Dundee while he took the other eight thousand to Perth where he stayed four days making his preparations, then moved south to intercept Edward. Word reached him that Edward had detached a force of some ten thousand men under Warren with orders to march on Stirling while he himself advanced towards Dundee. Wallace decided to meet this force and destroy it.

Chapter 10

The Battle of Falkirk

Wallace now rode to intercept Edward and the main army at Falkirk before they could cross the Forth nearby and invade Fife. This was a much more difficult task, the forces of the enemy greater and the king himself, a great field commander, in charge. Never had the cards been stacked so high against the Scots. But Wallace did his best to make the terrain work for him and used techniques which later helped Bruce to win Bannockburn against the second Edward, a fool compared to his father. He chose his ground carefully so that the marshes of the low ground protected the Scots in various places. He ordered pits to be dug and calthrops to be put in them, lightly covered with turf, to spike the horses' hooves. The cavalry he reckoned were to be feared most, but between marsh and calthrops he hoped to get them so bogged down they would be useless. His own small cavalry he did not, unlike Bruce, make the best of by keeping them in hand to scatter the English archery, who were in fact more dangerous in such terrain than cavalry. Did Wallace, whose success depended on guerrilla techniques really have to risk all in a major battle he couldn't possibly win? To him at any rate there seemed no real alternative. Knowing the importance of this battle, Scots flocked to him from all over, including Stewart of Bute and Lord Comyn. But Comyn had an old grudge against Wallace, and began to breed bad blood between him and Lord Stewart, saying that Stewart should be commander as Wallace was only a commoner. Wallace refused to give way and the Stewart faction, though they stayed and fought, were poisoned in their minds.

The Scots footmen were formed into a schiltrom, a square of spears several ranks deep, so that when one front line man fell another stepped forward to take his place. This was the main tactic which, together with exploiting marshy terrain and calthrops, was later to win Bannockburn. But there the cavalry also played an important role in scattering the English archers; here at Falkirk the cavalry were not so used to it and were overwhelmed in direct combat with their English opposite numbers. Stewart fought valiantly, his men so holding their ground that wave after wave of English cavalry foundered on the unsuitable ground and were broken on the iron ranks of the schiltrom. For a time it looked as though the Scots might prevail, and had proper use been made of the cavalry to ride down the English archers, as at Bannockburn, the day might have been won. But the Scots cavalry were scattered, rendered useless, and while the English cavalry could make no impression on the schiltrom, their archers soon did, pouring a hail of death from the air down on the unprotected spearmen. Wallace, unlike Bruce, had no way of breaking up the archers and they decided the outcome of the battle. One of the fiercest and most successful knights on the English side was Robert Bruce fighting his own subjects, shedding Scots blood in a battle against his own cause. Wallace was much aggrieved at this and very bitter about it. He himself had a divided sense of loyalty thus finding the man he was fighting to put on the throne his worst enemy in that cause. It is even said that the two men crossed swords in the battle, or that Bruce wounded his own best champion in the neck with a lance, causing him to retire from the field long enough to have the wound bound up lest he bled to death. It must have been a strange sight to see the lion rampant, the flag of Bruce, thus advanced against his own cause and people on behalf of the English tyrant Edward the First. What between that and the quarrel with Stewart, Wallace had vinegar enough to drink that day even before the bitter taste of defeat in battle. Edward himself did not take the field that day but left the fighting to his commanders, Hereford, the Bishop of Durham and Robert Bruce chief among them.

With the schiltrom broken by the archers and the cavalry destroying the remnants, Wallace decided on a bold plan; indeed he had little choice. Their only escape from annihilation lay in the Torwood and to reach it they must break through the ranks of Bruce's men. It was a do-or-die chance but Wallace never hesitated. He gathered all his horsemen together and charged full pelt into Bruce's army, not to fight, but to tear through. Fighting was necessary, but only in self-defence, and great havoc was wrought on Bruce's Englishry. The desperate gamble worked and Wallace's men got through, though leaving some of their number slain on the ground. The Bruce considered giving chase into the Torwood, but the English commander, the Earl of York, counselled him against it, for the Scots would have a stronghold in the forest. For the time being those who got through were safe.

Those who got through. But one of the noblest men in all Scotland was among those left dead on the field. An English knight noticed that Sir John Graham's corselet was too short, leaving a gap of waistline unarmed. He rode up from behind as Graham was carving his way through near Bruce himself and thrust a lance into his back, piercing his vital organs. The Graham at once spun round and slew the knight with a sword stroke, then slid off his horse to the ground, where the English closed in and finished him off with many wounds.

Once he saw his men safely on to the Torwood, Wallace rode back on the far side of the river Carron, and Bruce seeing him rode up to the edge of the river and shouted across to Wallace: 'Wallace, your deeds this day have won my admiration, I never saw such a man in the field, I would have words with you.' 'You,' said Wallace bitterly, 'who this day have slain your own subjects and betrayed your own cause, all I want of you is revenge.' But Bruce persisted and Wallace shouted, 'All right, say what you have to say. I can hear.' They rode a bit further along the river together, away from English ears. Bruce said, 'Wallace, why do you, who could easily have made peace with Edward, take such hardy warfare upon yourself. What do you want?' 'I'll tell you why, Carrick,' Wallace answered. 'Because you who ought to be doing so have betrayed your own cause and your own people. You are a traitor to Scotland, a disgrace to your name and destiny, and I despise you. No man who has fallen this day so that you can curry favour with your damned English king but is twice the man you are. You're not fit to kiss their feet, you who should be king. I hope your English master rewards his Scots dog with proper tit-bits for the day's villainy.' Bruce answered, 'War is war, and what you have lost this day is nothing to what you've done to us.' 'That's as it should be,' Wallace replied, 'and I would give you and all your traitor kind to see the Graham on his feet again. You have slain a man worth ten times all the rest of you false Scots nobles.' 'Look, Wallace,' said Bruce, 'I have a difficult and complicated game to play, but I would like nothing better than your service.' 'Your service, you dog, would you have me too fawning at the feet of your English master? I would be hanged first. But I have served manfully your own cause whose worst enemy you are.' Bruce said, 'Curb your tongue, man, I'm serious. You could rule all Scotland tomorrow with title, wealth and power if you would come into Edward's peace.' 'Edward's peace!' said Wallace. 'The only peace that criminal will ever get from me is at the point of a sword or the end of a rope. And you, too, Bruce, you devourer of your own blood, you despicable renegade. If I ever get my hands on you, by God you will fare worse at my hands than any accursed infidel Turk at the hands of a Christian knight. I could seize your crown, the crown of Scotland, in default of anybody fit to wear it, and that by right of arms. But I have not done so, because I respect the right of blood, the blood you dishonour with every vile breath you draw. It was a bad day for Scotland the day you were spawned on us.' By this time Wallace was in such a rage that Bruce laughed at his ardour, half in amusement, half in admiration. Serious again, he said, 'Wallace, you can see we have no chance in battle against the English might, our time is not yet. We have to be patient while he lives.' 'Speak for yourself,' Wallace replied. 'You have seen what I can do to his might. If all the nobles would take up the cause as I have done, what could we not do? I take my stand – a free Scotland or death.' Bruce was moved by the hero's passion. 'Wallace,' he said, 'I need your advice. Darkness is coming down now, but will you meet me to-morrow at nine in Dunipace chapel?' Wallace looked at him: 'And be betrayed to the English?' 'I give you my word on it, Wallace, I mean what I say, I want your advice,' and he crossed his right arm over his breast in vow of honour. Wallace looked at the young man born to be king of Scots. 'All right,' he said, 'but nine o'clock is too late, we'll be fighting by that time. Make it three in the morning. I'll bring ten men if you do the same.' 'I will,' said Bruce, 'and all of them Scots.'

They parted, and the Bruce rode back to Linlithgow where, eating his meal, he heard some English knights jeer at him in the very words of Wallace: 'Look how yon Scot eats his own blood.' Edward shut them up at once, not wanting his stooge offended, but Bruce scowled, and as he ate, he remembered all that Wallace had said to him, and his heart was heavy and troubled. He was indeed the true king of Scots, he had indeed eaten his own blood that day. His conscience gnawed at him and from that day he never again took the field against his own people.

Lament for the Graham

When Wallace arrived at the stronghold in the Torwood he found his men had rescued the corpse of the Graham and were gathered round it. When Wallace saw the body, the tears sprang to his eyes, and he leapt from his horse and took the Graham's head up in his arms, cradling it on his breast:

> He lighted down and took him from them all
> In his arms. Seeing the pale face
> He kissed him, crying often 'allace, allace,
> The best brother ever a man could get,
> My staunchest friend when I was most beset!
> My hope and hold, most honoured in this life,
> My faith, my ally, hardiest in strife!
> In thee was wit, freedom, and manliness;
> In thee was truth, courage and nobleness;
> In thee was rule, in thee was governance;
> In thee was virtue without variance;
> In thee was loyalty, open-handed dealing;
> Steadfastness in thee, and well-bred feeling;
> Greatly you fought for Scotland, freedom winning,
> Though I took up the cause in the beginning.
> I vow to God, who has the world in hold
> Your death shall be to the English dearly sold.
> You are martyred for Scotland's rights, and I
> Shall thee avenge, or in that cause will die.'

No man present at that scene, hearing Wallace thus lament, had a dry eye. Wallace then gave orders for the burial and began to prepare to meet the Bruce as promised. He chose his ten men and, as the night was already well on, rode off to that tryst.

Bruce was true to his word and the two men met as planned. When Wallace met Bruce, he shook with suppressed anger and desire for revenge. He greeted Bruce with a brutal attack: 'I have just come from burying a man worth any ten of you, dead through your villainy. It's as much as I can do to keep my hands off you. Are you not grovelling with shame at your treason, or are you beyond all hope of honour and decency, let alone majesty?' 'Grovelling, no,' said Bruce, 'but ashamed certainly. Your words hurt no more than my own conscience.' Wallace studied him closely and saw the truth stand in his eyes; the Bruce was won for Scotland, Scotland again would have a king. In his emotional state, Wallace was so deeply touched with gratitude to God that he knelt at Bruce's feet and said, 'My king, I thank God for it. Take up your kingdom, sire!' 'I will take up its saviour,' said Bruce and leant down to lift Wallace into his arms, and the two men embraced, Wallace frankly in tears, Bruce struggling to keep back his own. Wallace quickly recovered himself and said, 'My lord, leave that wicked king at once, don't go back, come and lead your own, we are all yours to command.' 'Wallace,' said Bruce, 'it's not quite so easy as that. Please try to understand the difficult position I am in at present. If I were to desert him at once I would break my bond and nobody would ever trust me again, it would bring even more disgrace on my kingship. I have to play a patient game meantime until something occurs which allows me to break with him without loss of honour – he must break the bond first. But I promise you before God and as the son of my father that never again will I lift a finger to help him against my own people. Believe me, Wallace, I will come to you and my people as soon as I possibly can, and my life thereafter in winning the kingdom and freeing my people from English domination will be my penance and apology for this day and every day I have taken arms for Edward against my own cause.'

Thus the two took leave of each other, Bruce with a heavy heart to rejoin the tyrant Edward, Wallace in haste to prepare for the next blow against him.

Edward Surprised at Linlithgow

Wallace divided his army into one half under Sir Malcolm and the other under his own command, each to approach Linlithgow from opposite sides, and by such routes as were not visible to the English sentinels. They reached the town without mishap and at a given signal fell on it at once. The English were taken completely by surprise in that early dawn and great havoc was wrought among them before they could assemble in any order. Edward himself was surprised and ordered Bruce and his men to take arms but Bruce refused to fight against the Scots and stood by watching like a referee. Edward did his best, rallying and inspiring his troops with the authority of the superb field commander he was, but with the Bruce faction taking no part the English were unequal to the struggle and the common soldiers began to flee in all directions, only the nobles battling on around their king. The town was now a blaze of burning houses as Earl Malcolm and his men went through it with fire and sword. Wallace and his chosen inner band hacked their way towards Edward himself, Wallace as usual reserving for himself the taking of the chief commander. In fact Wallace got so close to his hated enemy that he slew the standard-bearer in front of Edward's eyes, and at this the Earl of York, who with a band of nobles guarded the king's person, counselled Edward to flee the wrath of the battle-mad giant carving a way towards him. It was a bitter defeat for the old tiger to turn tail, but turn tail he did with curses of rage and frustration, and fled with the remaining two thirds of his army; the other third lay dead in and around Linlithgow. The Scots hastily mustered for the pursuit, those without horses and gear grabbing those left by the English. But they were in rather straggly disorder until Wallace called a halt, got them into some order, and rode on again.

Edward and his best-horsed guard got clean away but many of the less lucky English fell beneath the Scottish swords. But from that time on Bruce was a marked man. He had refused to fight, and when later challenged by Edward had asked to be released from his bond. From then on Bruce was practically a prisoner in England, kept under constant surveillance on Edward's orders. All Scots were withdrawn from him so that only Englishmen were his companions – or guards, rather. With Edward and the English gone, Dundee soon fell to the besiegers under Scrymgeour and, as promised, the captain was hanged in despite of the tyrant Edward, by Wallace's own orders.

Wallace Gives up His Command

Scotland was now once again comparatively at peace, and Wallace resigned his office, despite the entreaties of the lords, and decided to return to France to fight the English there. He had many adventures in France, and on the voyage over, his ship was attacked by an English pirate John of Lynn, and in the ensuing battle Wallace personally slew that scourge of Scottish ships. The king of France was delighted to see Wallace again and made him Duke of Guienne, which he soon cleared of the English invaders.

Meantime fate was spinning her web back in Scotland, where Sir John Menteith was meeting with that vile traitor Aylmer de Valence in Annan for a secret parley. De Valence persuaded Menteith, a name accursed for Wallace's sake in Scottish history, to come into Edward's pay. Menteith had an ambition to possess the Lennox, and having confided this to de Valence, it was easy for that man to tell him Edward would grant his wish and more for his help in subduing the Scots. They rode south together to meet King Edward who was only too pleased to receive another Scottish traitor, and to promise him all he wanted. This vile trading completed, Menteith returned to Scotland to await events and the opportunity to do his master's will.

He had not long to wait, for Edward was no sooner back in London than he started raising a bigger army than ever against the Scots, determined to crush them and be avenged on Wallace. He marched north, and this time, with Wallace gone, he met with no resistance. Not only was there no leader fit to take the place of Wallace but Menteith spread a rumour that Edward was coming to make Bruce king of Scots, and this so pleased most Scots that they felt no resistance was required. The hard core of Wallace's men made themselves scarce to avoid possible revenge and to see whether Menteith was telling the truth. They probably knew that liar better and were taking no chances. Edward therefore occupied the bulk of Scotland without fighting a battle. Some nobles who refused to come into his peace were sent to England, including Sir William Douglas, who died in prison there. Others took refuge in the isles and the far north. The traitors Corspatrick, John of Lorne and Comyn swore allegiance to Edward, as did many others. But the loyal nobles sent word to Wallace in France telling him of the new occupation, and begging him to come again to the rescue of his country, and assume the crown. For whatever reason, Wallace did not at once come running but stayed a while longer in France.

Edward meantime set up English lords over all the important Scottish castles and districts: York commanded the lands from Tay to Dee, Beaumont to the North, Clifford to Douglasdale, Comyn (a Scots renegade) to Galloway, Soulis to the Mearns, and so on. The good bishop Lamberton was still at St Andrews and James Douglas, the young son of Sir William Douglas, came to him from Paris. The good bishop, mistaking Edward's nature, thought to do the stripling good by presenting him to the king: as a result, because he was Sir William's son, Edward threw

James into jail. Having thus 'pacified' Scotland, Edward left it in the hands of his stooges and returned to London.

The Pact Between Bruce and Comyn

Now it happened that the Comyn had ambitions regarding Scotland which made him a somewhat unreliable ally of Edward: he had, after all, some claim to the throne himself. He now approached Bruce, who was still a semi-prisoner with Edward, and asked for a parley to which both would pledge secrecy. Bruce agreed, and the bond of secrecy sworn, Comyn then said, 'My lord, you know that you should by right be king of Scots.' Bruce said, 'Yes, I know, but this is not the time to press my legal right to the crown of Scotland. I am in the hands of my enemy who parcels out my kingdom to Englishmen and as wages for treason by renegade Scots.' Comyn then suggested that Bruce should cede his right to the crown to him in return for all the lands in Comyn hands. This Bruce refused, so Comyn then suggested that he would help Bruce become king in return for some suitable reward to be agreed upon later. He pointed out that Edward had given him all Galloway; Berwick to his nephew Soullis, and great highland estates to his nephew John of Lorn: all these would rise at Comyn's command in Bruce's cause if Bruce would come with him to Galloway. Bruce pondered this and said, 'If we could get Wallace back from France it would be worth considering, for that man could even now win back the kingdom from Edward. He and I have been too long apart: together we could achieve much.' On this tentative note they sealed a pact to rise together against Edward when the time was ripe. What happened thereafter is uncertain, but it is said that Comyn betrayed this secret to Edward in such terms as made Bruce only seem to be conspiring against Edward and seeking to throw in his lot with Wallace in a new rising.

Chapter 11

Wallace's Betrayal and Martyrdom

Wallace's exploits in France need not detain us. He had successes in Guienne, driving the English out; fought French adversaries and triumphed, and was so disgusted at being made to fight a lion, feeling it beneath a man to 'fecht a dog', that he left France in disdain. The French knights had been jealous of Wallace's superiority and the favour he found with the king, so that he became the object of murderous envy.

Wallace had an uneventful crossing from Sluys and landed at the mouth of the river Earn, whence he made his way to Elcho, meeting up with his cousin Crawford who soon told him of the dire state of Scotland. Crawford was living quietly and, unrecognised, could come and go among the English as much as he pleased. Wallace sent him to Perth to buy more provisions for himself and his men, but the English became suspicious at the quantity of goods he wanted and threw him in jail. They suspected that Wallace must be at the back of it, but Crawford declared that he wanted it for a marriage feast. The English didn't believe him, but decided to let him go and secretly follow him. They let him gather all the goods he wanted and set off with them: but scouts quietly followed behind, and behind them the whole town's force of some eight hundred men under young Butler. Wallace had had a bad dream about Crawford meantime, and greeted him with suspicion. Crawford told him what had happened, and Wallace immediately was on guard and sent out scouts to reconnoitre. They soon saw the array of English advancing slowly on the camp. As open battle was impossible Wallace ordered a retreat to Elcho Park, where they might have a better chance of defensive action. There was a dense patch of wood there in which a score of men, all they were, might manage to hold off a greater number and still make havoc among the attackers. To this end they quickly interwove many branches into a sort of palisade through or over which it would be very difficult for attackers to scramble, hampered by weapons and armour.

Young Butler soon saw the difficulty Wallace had placed him in, but he had an answer. Crawford's wife had been taken by the English in their advance, and they now brought her forward so that all the Scots could see her. They had tried to make her talk by threats and promises but she had not betrayed Wallace. Now Butler had a large fire built and his men prepared to throw her into it. This was too much for Wallace and he broke out from the stronghold shouting, 'You repulsive English cowards, do you make war on women? You should be ashamed of yourselves. Here I am, come and get me, if you're not too womanish to try.' Butler and his men rushed towards him and he let them come near before dodging back into the defence. The Scots were surrounded and fighting on all sides, but such was the difficulty of the place that numbers mattered little and those few English who got within reach of Scots swords never breathed again. Butler kept back a bit, dividing his men into groups attacking from all sides. Wallace kept his eye on him, but Butler gave him no opportunity to get at him. The English could make little impression on the Scots and Butler decided to play a waiting game and starve them out. Night fell, but the Scots had to keep up a vigilant watch, so they got little sleep.

Butler was hungry for revenge on Wallace, who had killed both his father and grandfather. The Earl of York was due to join Butler from Perth and Butler dearly wanted to have Wallace in his power before he arrived, or dead at his feet. So he thought he would try a little guile and rode up near the copse, shouting to Wallace that he wanted to speak to him and accused him of killing his father and grandfather. Wallace agreed, but pointed out that it was his duty to do so, as they would have killed him if they could, being traitors to Scotland. Butler then said that as Wallace could not possibly escape, he should yield to him and promised to spare his life. Wallace laughed him to scorn, saying it remained to be seen what would happen.

Next day the skirmishing began again, and by a ruse, Wallace managed to detract a lot of Butler's men to other parts of the fight, and watching his chance, dashed forth and carved a way to Butler, who stood his ground, offering defence. Wallace's mighty sword slew him at almost the first stroke. The Scots completely broke through the English ranks and made their escape to Methven Wood, leaving the English lamenting the death of yet another Butler at Wallace's hands.

Wallace had hoped that there would be plenty of food available in the forest, lots of wild animals to hunt, and indeed they managed to replenish their supplies. But it became clear that they could not stay there, so they pressed on next day to Birnam, and thence to Athol because Birnam was also sadly depleted. Wherever they went they found the English garrisons had plundered the countryside and the Scots were soon in serious trouble for lack of meat. Wallace was troubled that so many were going hungry in his cause, and he began to blame himself. He told his men to await his return and went off on his own, not with any plan in mind, but partly to think out what to do. He fell into a black mood of self-reproach, blaming himself for the plight of his men, even doubting the wisdom of his cause.

In this state of hunger and weariness he fell asleep under an oak tree. At forty-five, he was now beginning to age.

Now it chanced that the Earl of York had sent out five hand-picked men with strict orders, under pain of death, to track Wallace down and kill him. They had tracked him and his men all the way, and had followed him at a distance when he went off on his own. They now had a perfect chance to murder him in his sleep, but ambition stepped in. They thought how much better it would be if they took him alive and brought him back for the vengeance of the English, for Edward himself: they had visions of great rewards coming their way. So instead of slinking up and slaying him as he slept, they stole up and suddenly pounced on him to bind him. They might as well have done the same to a lion. The suddenness only intensified the power of Wallace's reaction as he hurled the men aside with a power they never expected and leapt to his feet. One man still clung to Wallace who simply dashed his brains out against the tree, at the same time grabbing his sword from him. A second man was slain at once, and the other three startled out of their minds by this phenomenon ran for it. Wallace was hard on their heels and struck down the nearest, then the next till all were dead. Then Wallace saw a youth standing nearby with a heavily loaded horse. The boy was petrified, and it turned out he was a Scot who had been conscripted into service of the enemy, and the horse was loaded with meat and provisions. Wallace reassured the boy and took him back with the provisions for his men. It was the first food they'd had for four days. Wallace's men were in two minds about how it had been acquired, for Wallace had never been in greater danger, and they chided him for going off without a bodyguard.

They returned to the lowlands in search of better provision and heard that things were just as bad there except within the English-held castles. One of these was Rannoch Hall, and they decided to attempt to take it, having been joined by some more willing men in their traipsing about the country. They silently approached the Hall and saw only one man standing guard at the door. Not wishing him to raise the alarm, he was quietly seized and silenced with a hand over his mouth and, thus struggling, was hauled away to the main body. They were about to kill him when he managed to hiss that he was a Scot, so they spared him and quizzed him about the set-up inside the Hall. It turned out that there were no English in the Hall but only a Scots lord who had been forced to make peace with Edward. Hearing this and led by the man, Wallace and his men walked boldly up to the door which Wallace burst in with one mighty kick and strode inside. He was recognised at once, and the lord leapt forward glad to meet him. Wallace was back! He gave thanks to God, and all were made welcome and feasted well into the night.

Things were still very difficult for Wallace, as he wandered about more like an outlaw than a potential conqueror, waiting his chance, in dire straits, looking for food and gear. Meantime de Valence was working away at Menteith to get Wallace into English hands. Now Wallace at this time had no reason to believe that Menteith was a traitor, because part of that man's strategy was to curry favour with the Scots in such small ways as he could, so that Wallace had reason to think him one of those who would rise when the opportunity came. But Menteith saw that this time Wallace could not work the miracle, and he planned his own advancement with the conquering English. Wallace's magic had gone. Yet Menteith had qualms about bringing about the death of this great man, and de Valence tried to dispel these by promising him that Edward only wanted to imprison Wallace, and keep him out of mischief. In addition, he promised Menteith Dumbarton castle and paid him three thousand pounds gold, at sight of which Menteith's scruples melted away. He also promised the lordship of the Lennox, which he had long coveted.

Thus Menteith bound himself to Edward to deliver Wallace into his hands as and when he could, it being understood he was not to be slain but kept in prison in England. Such is the power of greed and lust for power. De Valence rode off south to show Edward the pact he had made with Menteith, which was joyously received. Menteith meantime had his own nephew infiltrate the Wallace camp in the guise of a patriotic Scot, to keep his uncle posted on the hero's movements and plans.

Wallace realised that he had done all he could for Scotland, it was time for the nobles to take over from a commoner like himself. He therefore wrote to Robert Bruce, reminding him of his duty and pleading with him to come and take the crown. Bruce replied thanking Wallace for his loyalty and virtue, saying that he would indeed come north soon, he was simply waiting an opportunity to slip his guards and escape. He asked Wallace to meet him secretly near Glasgow on the first of July. He was sure that Comyn had betrayed him and he was likely to be accused at the coming English parliament, and that would give him reason to disregard his bond and escape to Scotland. Wallace was delighted and moved into the Glasgow vicinity to await the coming of the rightful heir to the throne. It is said that round about this time Wallace met Edward Bruce, Robert's brother, who was busy in his mother's cause in Ireland, and Wallace did homage to him as next in line to his brother's throne. But all these matters were reported to Menteith who realised he must act before Wallace and Bruce met up, or it would be too late. He therefore hurried to Glasgow with a few score handpicked, bribed men.

Wallace's tryst with Bruce was near Robroyston, and it was there he had camped with a few of his closest men – and the traitor. Robroyston at this time was one house and little else, and Wallace was able to use the house, in friendly hands, as his own. The traitor waited till Wallace was asleep then slunk off to tell his uncle Menteith. He had previously hidden the arms of Wallace and Kerlie, the one man with him in the house, so there was little danger. The house was soon surrounded and the traitor opened the door to Menteith's men. The sleeping men had no chance, Kerlie was killed at once but they wanted Wallace alive so a great struggle ensued in which the big man brained one against the wall and broke another's back: but they managed to get him down and bind his hands. Even then, Wallace was a handful, kicking and threshing with his legs so that they could not bind them. But Menteith pretended that he was in fact saving him from the English and taking him not to Edward but to Clifford, who had no desire to kill Wallace if he would promise to stop making war. Wallace had trusted Menteith, and was half-inclined to believe him, but he had little choice now anyway. So at last he allowed himself to be led out. Menteith also told him that, as the English were all round outside, it must seem that he, Menteith, had taken Wallace prisoner and they could safely leave matters in his hands. Once outside, Wallace saw there were no English but by then it was too late. Thus, waiting to meet his king, a meeting which would have changed all Scottish history, Wallace was betrayed to the English, and Bruce's road made three times as hard as it would have been had Wallace been his general. He was delivered to de Valence who marched him barefoot to London via Carlisle at the back of a horse. The terrible vengeance of these frightened men whom Wallace had terrorised had begun.

When the news got round, all Scotland wept for the loss of their deliverer. De Longville swore vengeance for Wallace, and later joined Bruce, doing great service in his cause. Bruce himself arrived only four days after, too late to save his faithful warrior, and his grief and frustration knew no limits: he had counted on Wallace being his main guarantee of success against the English, but now he was alone, with only his wayward brother Edward. Ah, Bruce, had you but come to Wallace at the right time, what a different tale there would have been. With you as king and Wallace your faithful general, what could you not have done together for Scotland! But Scottish history is punctuated throughout with such sighs: IF ONLY... If Wallace had had his army with him it could never have happened; but it was part of the agreement with Bruce that each should be almost alone.

The rest is soon told. Bruce was somewhat delayed because he trysted with Comyn in a church near Dumfries on his way north, charged him with his treason, and then in a rage murdered him in the church – an act of sacrilege which dogged him till his dying day and in the end cost Douglas his life and Scotland her next best leader. Wallace was taken to Westminster and there charged with treason in a court consisting of the Lord Chief Justice, Mallory, and a number of other English peers. The trial was a travesty, Wallace's guilt being assumed. A great list of his crimes was read out to him, each one rousing cries of hate and anger from the English audience. Wallace asked for a defence lawyer but was simply shouted down. Seeing that his 'trial' was a farce, Wallace denounced it as such and refused to take any further part in it. But when at the end of his list of crimes, which included those against the church, he was accused of treason against Edward, he broke his statuesque silence to say, 'I have never betrayed Edward, nor any other English lord, for I never submitted to them. You cannot break a word you never gave, and my allegiance is and always has been to the legitimate king of Scots and to Scotland. Edward is a tyrant, a usurper, and a criminal fit only for the rope.' And he spat on the floor. The English lords were driven to insensate rage at this, but Wallace never spoke again. When the hubbub died down the atrocious sentence was read out, slowly, lingeringly, but the big man never blinked an eyelid.

The farce over, Wallace was dragged outside where a huge crowd waited, jeering and cursing. There was a large company of mounted gentry to lead the procession. There was a horse with a sort of gate trailing at its back, about as broad as a man, the harnessed end some two or three feet from the ground, the other end trailing on the ground. The jailers now tore the clothes off Wallace till he was stark naked, and he was bound to the gate, feet up, head down bumping on the ground. A party of young men armed with sticks fell in behind Wallace and to the shouts and cries of the crowd the procession set off for Smithfield, the young men hammering Wallace with the sticks as they went. When he lost consciousness under the beating, and the stones and rubbish thrown by the crowd, his head bumped along on the filthy road covered with horse dung. He was half-dead, but still half conscious when they arrived at the scaffold and he was unbound (except for his hands which were still pinioned behind him at the wrists) and helped to his feet by the hangman's aides. Wallace shouted for a priest to confess his sins to, but Edward, who sat with some lords and ladies on a stand built for the occasion, forbade this. Wallace then shouted that his psalter, which he always carried with him about his person, or any psalter, should be held open before his eyes. The archbishop of Canterbury intervened as Edward was about to forbid this too, and came forward to shrive the doomed man. Edward threatened to have him arrested if he dared to do this, but the archbishop retorted he would have Edward excommunicated if he did. The archbishop then heard Wallace's confession, insofar as he was able to give it, and a priest came forward with the psalter. Wallace was now helped up the steps of the scaffold and stood between his attendants, swaying, having to be held up. The hangman, in his grim uniform and black mask, was almost as huge a giant as Wallace himself, with mighty bare arms. A brazier was burning ready on the scaffold; the rope hanging at head-height. The hangman fixed the rope round Wallace's neck and the big man was dragged up off the ground. When he had dangled writhing and twitching for about two minutes he was let down, unconscious but still alive, and dumped on the scaffold. The hangman now took out his knife and castrated Wallace, throwing his sexual parts into the fire. He then slit his belly open and drew out his entrails, throwing them also onto the fire: this was said to be for his crimes against the church. Then the great heart was cut out of the breast and held aloft for the roaring crowd to see. The hangman now took an axe and cut off first one leg, then the other, then the arms, and finally the head, which also he held up for the crowd. Never had they seen such a head, nor ever would again. The sport was now over. The head was fixed on Tower Bridge, the limbs at Newcastle, Berwick, Stirling and Perth. So died the saviour of Scotland. But in Scotland Bruce was taking up the cause, and Wallace had his triumph when his spirit rode with its king, Robert Bruce, on the field of Bannockburn.

Scots Wha Hae

Scots, wha hae wi Wallace bled,
Scots, wham Bruce has aften led,
Welcome to your gory bed,
Or to victorie!

Now's the day, and now's the hour,
See the front o' battle lour;
See approach proud Edward's power –
Chains and slaverie!

Wha will be a traitor-knave?
Wha can fill a coward's grave?
Wha sae base as be a slave?
Let him turn and flee!

Wha for Scotland's king and law
Freedom's sword will strongly draw,
Freeman stand, or freeman fa',
Let him follow me!

By oppression's woes and pains!
By your sons in servile chains!
We will drain our dearest veins,
But they shall be free!

Lay the proud usurpers low!
Tyrants fall in ev'ry foe!
Liberty's in ev'ry blow! –
Let us do – or die!

Robert Burns